MUTUAL MINDFULNESS

NLP & AIKIDO

THE STUDY OF THE UNIVERSAL PRINCIPLES OF EXCELLENCE

BY

PADDY BERGIN

Copyright © 2018 by Paddy Bergin

All rights reserved. This book or any portion thereof may not be reproduced or used in any manner whatsoever without the express written permission of the publisher except for the use of brief quotations in a book review.

Printed in the United Kingdom

First Printing, 2018

ISBN 978-1-5272-2337-0

Mutual Mind Publishing

London

www.mutualmindfulness.com

Front & Back Cover Design:

markreeveillustrator.com

Dedicated to:
Dolan and Matt Bergin

The concepts, strategies and tools in this book are transferable and get results.

The book is designed so you can read any chapter and immediately apply the key ideas to your life and business, getting immediate results.

Be a yardstick of quality. Some people aren't used to an environment where excellence is expected.

– Steve Jobs

ACKNOWLEDGEMENTS

When Helen Keller was accused of plagiarism, her friend Mark Twain wrote her a lively letter of support, in which he asserted that:

"All ideas are second-hand, consciously and unconsciously drawn from a million outside sources" and that "the kernel, the soul... the actual and valuable material of all human utterances is plagiarism."

I would like to thank the many people who have encouraged and supported me during the long process of putting this book together including the following:

Robert Dilts, Judy Delozier, Andy Hathaway Sensei, Jochen Encke, Bill Atkinson, Lyn Cooper, Adie De Coursey, Carol Howley, Bill Howley, Anand Rao, Lizel Louw, Keith Bentley, Kamaey Sodhi, Aya Phipps, Julian Russell, Glen Savage, Matthew Huggins, Riki Moss, Phil Croskin, Kim Griffiths, Peter Gray, Sorel Radu, Claire Lauder, Nick Owen, Andrew Godelman, Simon Horton, Andrea Foa, Karl Lancaster Sensei, Paulo Corralini Shihan, Ulf Evanas Shihan, Mike Cunningham, Sophie Blogs, Steve Langley, Jo Wheeler, Henry Devine, Janice Hemmings, Alan Cowie, Tristan Soames, Keith Meredith, Ursula Grunewald, Simon Beer.

FOREWORD

This is a very interesting and groundbreaking book. Take an esoteric and demanding Japanese martial art with ancient origins and marry it up with a modern scheme for modeling excellence valued in business, therapeutic and educational circles, and to then argue convincingly that they are the same thing, came from the same source, is both bold and novel.

Reading it may help progress along the Aikido pathway, or elucidate NLP, or both.

It's very much a win win perspective. If you like, enjoy, identify with what is said, it cannot help but take you forward. If you find the argument does not ring true or accord with your own experience, that process will inevitably bend your mind and senses and equally take you forward.

It needs to be read, re-read and above all practiced (a keynote of the book).

Words and ideas without the grounding of practice are at best hollow?

– Andy Hathaway, Dojo Cho, The London Aikido Club

Table of Contents

ACKNOWLEDGEMENTS 5
FOREWORD 7
PREFACE 11
   Aikido In Action 11
INTRODUCTION 17
CHAPTER 1 – EXCELLENCE 25
   What is Excellence? 25
   What is NLP? 30
   Neuro-Logical Levels 36
   Interruption 41
CHAPTER 2 – AIKIDO 45
   Mapping Across 50
CHAPTER 3 – LEARN LIKE A BABY 69
   Know what you want 80
   The Process of "Reframing" 84
   How we feel will determine how well we perform 85
   Well Forming an Outcome 89
   Awareness 91
   Flexibility 98
   Learning 99
   Thinking and Influence 104
   Thinking about Thinking 114
   Changing Bad Memories 122
CHAPTER 4 – THE PRESUPPOSITIONS OF NLP 127
CHAPTER 5 – AWARENESS 143
   Awareness 148
   Avoiding Street Robbery & Curing Back Pain 162
   Peripheral Vision 165
CHAPTER 6 – BECOME THE ENEMY 167
   Perceptual Positions, a Triple description 167

Characterlogical Adjectives – a Perceptual Position Exercise 171
  Communicating with your Unconscious Mind 178
  Daydream to Success 183
CHAPTER 7 – RELATIONSHIP & NON-CONFLICT 189
  Aikido – The Way of the Sword with no Sword 197
  The Principle of Matching 200
  The Brain Gym and The Structure of Influence 210
CHAPTER 8 – GETTING IN A STATE 215
  Anchoring – Does the name Pavlov ring a Bell? 226
  Anchoring Exercise 227
CHAPTER 9 – POWER 231
  Power is The ability to act or produce an effect 231
  Centering 233
  Centering Exercise 234
  Centering for a Challenging Situation 237
CHAPTER 10 – JOINING THE DOTS 239
  Pattern learning and the importance of relationship 244
  Conclusion 248
  Back to Basics 250
CHAPTER 11 – CURIOSITY 253
REFERENCES 259
GLOSSARY 273
APPENDICES 279
  Predicates 279
  The Self Hypnosis Technique 286
  What to do and how to do it 290
  Universal Principles of Excellence 296

PREFACE

"The Art of Peace is the principle of non-resistance. Because it is non-resistant it is victorious from the beginning. Those with evil intentions or contentious thoughts are vanquished. The Art of Peace is invincible because it contends with nothing."
– O Sensei.

AIKIDO IN ACTION

"Doing Combat with the Essence of Love" by Terry Dobson

The train clanked and rattled through the suburbs of Tokyo on a drowsy spring afternoon and our car was comparatively empty – a few housewives with their kids, some old folks going shopping. I gazed absently at the drab houses and dusty hedgerows.

At one station the doors opened, and suddenly a man bellowing violent, incomprehensible curses shattered the afternoon quiet. The man staggered into our car. He wore labourer's clothing, and he was big, drunk, and dirty. Screaming, he swung at a woman holding a baby. The blow sent her spinning into the laps of an elderly couple. It was a miracle that the baby was unharmed.

Terrified, the couple jumped up and scrambled toward the other end of the car. The labourer aimed a kick at the retreating back of the old woman but missed as she scuttled to safety. This so enraged the drunk that he grabbed the metal pole in the center of the car and tried to wrench it out of its stanchion. I could see that one of his hands was cut and bleeding. The train lurched ahead, the passengers frozen with fear. I stood up.

I was young then, some twenty years ago, and in pretty good shape. I'd been putting in a solid eight hours of aikido training nearly every day for the past three years. I liked to throw and grapple. I thought I was tough. Trouble was, my martial skill was untested in actual combat. As students of aikido, we were not allowed to fight.

"Aikido," my teacher had said again and again, "is the art of reconciliation. Whoever has the mind to fight has broken his connection with the universe. If you try to dominate people, you are already defeated. We study how to resolve conflict, not how to start it."

I listened to his words and I tried hard to live up to his instruction. I even went so far as to cross the street to avoid the chimpira, the pinball punks who lounged around the train stations. My forbearance exalted me. I felt both tough and holy. In my heart, however, I wanted an absolutely legitimate opportunity whereby I might save the innocent by destroying the guilty.

"This is it!" I said to myself as I got to my feet. People are in danger. If I don't do something fast, somebody will probably get hurt.

Seeing me stand up, the drunk recognized a chance to focus his rage. "Aha!" he roared. "A foreigner! You need a lesson in Japanese manners!"

I held on lightly to the commuter strap overhead and gave him a slow look of disgust and dismissal. I planned to take this turkey apart, but he had to make the first move. I wanted him mad, so I pursed my lips and blew him an insolent kiss. "All right!" he hollered. "You're gonna get a lesson." He gathered himself for a rush at me.

A split second before he could move, someone shouted "Hey!" It was ear splitting. I remember the strangely joyous, lilting quality of it – as though you and a friend had been searching diligently for something and he had suddenly stumbled upon it. "Hey!"

I wheeled to my left; the drunk spun to his right. We both stared down at a little old Japanese. He must have been well into his seventies, this tiny gentleman, sitting there immaculate in his kimono. He took no notice of me but beamed delightedly at the labourer, as though he had a most important, most welcome secret to share.

"C'mere," the old man said in an easy vernacular, beckoning to the drunk. "C'mere and talk with me." He waved his hand lightly.

The big man followed, as if on a string. He planted his feet belligerently in front of the old gentleman and roared above the clacking wheels, "Why the hell should I talk to you?" The drunk now had his back to me. If his elbow moved so much as a millimetre, I'd drop him in his socks.

The old man continued to beam at the labourer. "What'cha been drinkin'?" he asked, his eyes sparkling with interest.

"I been drinkin' sake," the labourer bellowed back, "and it's none of your business!" Flecks of spittle spattered the old man.

"Oh, that's wonderful," the old man said, "absolutely wonderful! You see I love sake too. Every night, me and my wife, (she's 76, you know), we warm up a little bottle of sake and take it out into the garden, and we sit on an old wooden bench. We watch the sun go down, and we look to see how our persimmon tree is doing. My great-grandfather planted that tree, and we worry about whether it will recover from those ice storms we had last winter. Our tree has done better than I expected though, especially when you consider the poor quality of the soil. It is gratifying to watch when we take our sake and go out to enjoy the evening – even when it rains!" He looked up at the labourer, eyes twinkling.

As he struggled to follow the old man's conversation the drunk's face began to soften. His fists slowly unclenched. "Yeah," he said, "I love persimmons too…" His voice trailed off.

"Yes," said the old man, smiling. "And I'm sure you have a wonderful wife."

"No," replied the labourer. "My wife died." Very gently, swaying with the motion of the train, the big man began to sob. "I don't got no wife, I don't got no home, I don't got no job. I'm so ashamed of myself." Tears rolled down his cheeks; a spasm of despair rippled through his body.

Now it was my turn. Standing there in my well-scrubbed youthful innocence, my "make this world safe for democracy" righteousness, I suddenly felt dirtier than he was.

Then the train arrived at my stop. As the doors opened, I heard the old man cluck sympathetically. "My, my," he said. "That is a difficult predicament, indeed. Sit down here and tell me about it."

I turned my head for one last look. The labourer was sprawled on the seat, his head in the old man's lap. The old man was softly stroking the filthy, matted hair.

As the train pulled away, I sat down on a bench. What I had wanted to do with muscle had been accomplished with kind words. I had just seen aikido tried in combat, and the essence of it was love. I would have to practice the art with an entirely different spirit. It would be a long time before I could speak about the resolution of conflict.

> Terry Dobson trained at Hombu Dojo in Tokyo from 1960 – 1969 under O Sensei, Morihei Ueshiba, the founder of Aikido. His story is reprinted here by kind permission of Riki Moss

When I first started Aikido training over 30 years ago I came across this now well-known story written by an American Aikidoka about an incident that he witnessed and the learning he got from that situation and now 30 years later I understand just how much is contained in this story.

Later, after we have been through some of the principles of excellence, we will begin to analyse this story and discover the structure of what the old man did to deal with the angry, drunk man in the story in such a dramatic way.

Hopefully, what you will realise as you read this book is that you are already using a lot of these principles, albeit unconsciously, and perhaps this book will bring to your conscious awareness the many ways you can utilise the principles of excellence even more purposefully.

I am presupposing that you, the reader, are curious to know the principles of excellence that I am talking about.

Some of you will want to know straight away and get on with it and some of you will find that this is what you are waiting for and would like to go through the book and take time to consider these principles.

For those of you who usually just want to get on with things I have made a list of the principles at the end of the book on page 296/297. When you get there and read through the list, you may find that you are then curious to know how specifically you can use these principles to help you deal with whatever is holding you back and help you achieve what you want.

For me, I guess, I am more big picture oriented and once I have got the framework or edges, as in a jigsaw puzzle, I will then begin to fill in the detail, the content, so I can understand someone wanting to know all the principles first, immediately, and then having done that come back for more information.

INTRODUCTION

"People don't write music. It's given to them"
— Hank Williams

One day, not long ago, I was standing on a Tube train waiting for it to pull into Moorgate Station in the City of London and as I was standing there I was sort of planning my speech for the launch party of this book long before I either had finished the book or had a publishing deal. I was visualising my own future success, a strategy that you will find out even more about later in this book, when a thought came to mind.

Interesting phrase, isn't it? How specifically did it, that thought, "come to mind" and who knows how these connections are made that can create thoughts, seemingly out of the blue (another interesting phrase), maybe intuition, yes. Or perhaps the feel of the train swaying as we were travelling through the tunnels and the sound of the metal wheels on the track bouncing off the brick walls of the tunnels as well as the whirr of the train motors helped me go into an altered or trance state and allowed my unconscious mind to take the opportunity to present these thoughts.

I was reminded of interviews I had seen and heard on TV and Radio and I'm sure a lot of you will have also seen, heard or read about these sorts of interviews with famous and successful songwriters such as Paul McCartney, John Lennon, Van Morrison, Bjork and most recently Keith Richards during an interview about his new solo album. When they were asked how they wrote their songs they pretty much all said the same thing.

The song sort of found them. It appeared somehow and they had to grab it while it was there or someone else, like Robert Plant, as Keith Richards said, might come along and get it instead.

He said: "It was out there and was channelled through me and I just had to write it down."

Leonard Cohen said:

"If I knew where the good songs came from, I'd go there more often."

Paul McCartney said he woke up with the melody of "Yesterday" in his head and it has now been covered over 3000 times by other artists.

Van Morrison does not consider himself a songwriter but is channelling ideas that are coming through him from the ether and later saying that: *"Jung's theory of the collective unconscious is the closest expression I can find for my work."*

Jimmy Webb, writer of the classic song "Wichita Lineman" that became hugely successful for Glen Campbell, said that the song came so easily it was almost like a wind blew through the room and left the song on the piano.

Icelandic singer, Bjork, describes her song writing as a spiritual experience.

Ed King, who was the bass player in the southern rock band Lynyrd Skynyrd, before switching to lead guitar, said that the night before the band recorded their classic song; *"Sweet Home Alabama"*, he had a dream during which he heard the two guitar solos note for note.

Austin Richman, Musician and Yoga Teacher says:

"Inspiration and/or meaning also starts to eek out of seemingly unrelated experiences which allow the magic of the muse to guide you through all areas of your life rather than when you are just sitting down with instrument in hand."

In the words of Steve Jobs:

"Creativity is just connecting things. When you ask creative people how they did something, they feel a little guilty because they didn't really do it. They just saw something. It seemed obvious to them after a while. That's because they were able to connect experiences they've had and synthesise new things."

One of the most famous examples of this "magical" song writing process comes from Keith Richards himself. He said he always had a tape recorder by his bedside and one morning he woke up and noticed the tape recorder had run the tape to the end on record. When he rewound it and pressed play he heard himself humming the first verse and playing the riff of "Satisfaction" followed by 45 minutes of snoring, and we all know how successful and long lasting that song became and still is.

NLP (Neuro Linguistic Programming) developer, Robert Dilts, modelled Mozart's composing strategy and wrote about it in his book series "Strategies of Genius". Robert discovered how Mozart would go for a walk after a nice meal and during that walk or while travelling in a carriage his ideas flowed best and he did not know where they came from.

Mozart experienced his senses at the same time, an ability known as synesthesia, when you can hear a piece of music and simultaneously have a feeling, or feel frightened when looking down from a great height and this process was like an unconscious dream state to him and he was able to see the whole musical piece, not as musical notes but rather something like an abstract painting.

I had a similar experience writing this book. After I had been training in Aikido and NLP for some years I began to notice that the principles in both fields were the same and I made some notes on scraps of paper. At that time I did not have any plan to write a book but the pile of notes grew bigger and bigger and finally I decided to collate the notes into some sort of document for my own ease of reference.

I gathered the scraps of paper together, scanned through them and began to write a sort of overview of the notes.

What I wrote was a piece that was 7000 words long and it became the essence or heart of this book. At that time I thought that was all I was going to write but the ideas and notes kept coming and they eventually became the beginnings of a book that began to grow and grow. I had not planned to write a book, it sort of found me and like the songwriters and Mozart I was compelled to write it down and what I wrote was the "Big Picture" of the whole book. As I said, I do prefer or even need to have the outline first, like building the sides of a jigsaw puzzle and then filling in the inside or content. Other people work better with detail and fit things together as you go.

As Judy Delozier says: *"The goose is out of the bottle."*

NLP has long had ways of opening doors to the unconscious using the strategies developed in NLP New Code by Judy Delozier and John Grinder in the 1980s and some scientific explanation of the seemingly "magical" insights that can be gained from using these processes come later in this book.

So, what would be important to you right now about knowing the universal principles of excellence so that you can follow and utilise them easily to enable you to perform even more effectively and achieve what you want? What difference does that make to and for you?

The process of being excellent has a structure and certain principles, which when we utilise them in whatever we are doing, enable us to succeed.

It is not about the content of what we are doing but the process of how we do things. I am a NLP Coach amongst other things and I have coached and trained people in Corporate Banks, Project Management, and Education in Colleges, Universities and a consulting job in a London inner city school which was an eye opener, Premier League football teams, Training Companies, Charities, Local Government, NGOs and Aikido.

I have a coaching practice where people come to see me for help in sorting out and looking for solutions to their problems and learning strategies so that they can clear any blocks they might have, be happier and even more effective in their lives. I never know what they will bring until we meet and I never predict what I will do with them. I simply listen and I mean really listen and watch and then respond to whatever is in front of me at the time.

In Aikido this response to what is in front of you is called Awase, where you match and blend with whatever the other person is doing.

"Most people do not listen to understand; They listen with the intent to reply". – Stephen R Covey

I don't have to be an expert in all of these areas to deliver the universal principles of excellence but I do need a set of tools that allow me to model and work with the strategies that my client is employing.

The players in a Premier League Football (Soccer) team are elite athletes and what makes the difference between them is in their thinking, their state of mind and their ability to use their skills to work as a high performing generatively creative team, rather than just their physical skills. The same would apply to the managers and coaches.

Acquiring and utilizing both physical and mental skills in a particular way enables you to step up a level in your learning and spontaneously generate new behaviours.

Most conflict you will ever have is going to be within yourself, so learn to deal with yourself, to be mindful of your thinking process in an ongoing manner, monitoring what you are feeling and what happened for you to feel like that and be able to learn to choose how you want to feel.

My outcome is that this book will be a "Manual for Life". Our brains don't come with a manual but some very smart and successful people have already been there, modeled and unpacked the structure of our thinking and how we can make adjustments to our own internal representations so as to either, deal with problems, enhance positive feelings or motivate ourselves to build compelling futures, i.e. goals and as you read this book you will discover some very effective and proven ways to do this.

The principles of excellence discussed in this book do not only apply to Aikido and NLP but to anything we do, any skill(s) we are learning and using in any context.

CHAPTER 1 – EXCELLENCE

Experts are made not born

WHAT IS EXCELLENCE?

According to The Oxford English Dictionary the word excellence comes from the Latin word *excellentia*, which is from the verb excellere 'to surpass'.

Psychologist, Dr K Anders Ericsson defines excellence as the role of deliberate practice in the acquisition of expert performance. His emphasis is on practice, rather than intelligence and talent, which no amount of training will develop.

Deliberate practice involves two kinds of learning: improving the skills you already have and extending the reach and range of your skills. All the evidence shows that experts are always made, not born.

Excellence is a quality that is unusually good and so surpasses ordinary standards. It is also used as a standard of performance as measured. Ericsson introduced the idea that 10,000 hours of practice is necessary to become expert or masterly in any skill or performance. His more recent research has investigated how "deliberate practice" leads to exceptional performance.

However, what sort of practice and importantly, how we practice can accelerate the learning process or keep us always just short of what is possible. This book is about making available to anyone interested in significant improvement, those skills, both, physical and cognitive, necessary to perform in an excellent way. The way of being excellent, if you will, and In NLP terms that way is "The Difference that makes the Difference".

Famous Japanese swordsman, Miamoto Musashi said:

"From one thing know ten thousand things. Knowing the principles of 'Heiho' (literally the path to enlightenment) will give you the understanding to anything. Take what one knows and apply it to other things. Don't just learn, apply your learning to whatever you do."

So what are these principles and how can we use them?

Have you ever had the experience of very nearly giving up on something but suddenly got so determined about it, you carried on, completed and succeeded in whatever you were doing? How did you do that? What's the structure of your determination and how do you motivate yourself to persevere?

Perhaps you have had an example of working with your team whether it's in sports, a business project or socially and communication was breaking down, people weren't listening to each other and you were all pretty much stuck. Then you remembered something you did with a problem amongst your family or friends, a time when you had managed to turn around the situation and you then used that strategy with your team and a solution was found. Here you are looking and stepping outside the situation to gain access to new ideas that hadn't previously been available to you in this particular context.

What about a time when you found that you had an unexplainable good feeling or the times you chose to think of a special event in your life because it makes you feel so good in the present.

These are "moments of unconscious excellence" and I think we all have some "moments" like this and they are in fact available to anyone at any time. A solution emerges and often it may seem like its not you doing it or saying it and it just happens in that "moment". Like the songwriters said, when asked how they get their ideas, that it doesn't feel as if they are writing the song, it comes from somewhere else and they just have to write it down. It's almost as if they are getting out of their own way.

Very occasionally when I have been doing Aikido and have responded to an attack, my uke (training partner) goes flying and I wonder if I did that because it feels like I haven't done anything. That was probably a rare moment when I must have blended so well with their movement or more probably their intention that there was no clash of power, no conflict and I was able to put them in a position where they couldn't avoid falling.

You've probably had the experience of pushing on a door to open it and at that moment someone opened it from the other side and you found yourself stumbling forward. It's remarkable how much energy there is contained in that little push and because of the expectation of some resistance and the surprise when there isn't any we can't help falling forward.

I once lived in a first floor flat, just off the Holloway Road in North London and the windows overlooked the street and the houses on the other side. Most Saturday nights there was a party in the house opposite with lots of people coming and going. Something happened inside the house one time and I was attracted by the noise of people shouting, Police sirens wailing and blue lights flashing.

When I looked out my window I could see several police vehicles in the street and a lot of officers standing at the top of the steps up to the front door and another Police Officer emerging from the house and struggling to get a young man through the door.

The Police Officer must have got a bit frustrated with the young man and gave him a hearty push from behind and at that moment the young man turned sideways to respond to a friend shouting to him from the street level outside and the Policeman went stumbling forward, just like when you push a door as its opened from the other side, and he rolled down the steps coming to a stop on the pavement.

Perfect timing but unfortunately for the young man the other Police officers assumed he had caused the officer's fall and several of them immediately jumped on him and pinned him to the ground.

So those "moments" actually contain a structure that can be unpacked, modelled and learnt by others and we can and are doing this in both NLP and Aikido.

As William Blake said in his poem "To See a World…"

> To see a World in a Grain of Sand
> And a Heaven in a Wild Flower,
> Hold Infinity in the palm of your hand
> And Eternity in an hour

Richard Bandler describes NLP as the ability to "Break the chains such as fear, sadness and hate". These chains are made up of negative feelings, limiting beliefs and destructive behaviours. Freedom from these chains is about having flexibility in your behaviour and the ability to change your own internal state, i.e. how you feel.

I started writing notes on the similarities between NLP and Aikido in 2003, mostly because I saw, heard and continually bumped into the same ideas and principles in each field. I'd be on the mat in the Dojo training and listening to instructions about connecting and leading while also being told to maintain my own posture, balance and awareness of what is going on around me.

I'd say to myself: "Wow that sounds just like NLP". This book is the result of the notes that were an on-going record of some of my thoughts as I trained in both disciplines and began to not only connect the two fields but also realise that these are universal principles, which can be applied by anyone in any context to avoid conflict, deal with problems, perform excellently and achieve your outcomes.

I was studying two separate disciplines and was able to step up a level and see and experience the bigger picture of the skills necessary to perform anything in an excellent way.

Let me say something about jargon. Sometimes when I have been delivering NLP Training someone complains about the Jargon being used, particularly if you are in the UK, because two American guys developed NLP and, as you know some of their words are different, for example, the use of the word outcome instead of goal.

My response to that is yes it is unfamiliar, initially, and every field or discipline has its own jargon. When we are training in Aikido all the techniques have Japanese names and we count in Japanese. It is not that we are trying to be Japanese; it is just the way it is. The positive aspect to this is that I can go anywhere in the world and train in a local dojo, and I have done that, and I will hear those same words and be able to understand and follow what's going on. The same goes for NLP.

WHAT IS NLP?

Neuro Linguistic Programming (NLP) is often defined as the study of excellence or the difference between competence and excellence. This process of studying excellence is called "modelling" and is the heart of NLP and from the initial studies made by the founders has come many applications, including skills useful for the modelling process itself.

NLP is focusing on **what** works rather than **why** it works.

Here's a definition I came across:

"NLP has evolved as an innovative technology enabling the practitioner to organise information and perceptions in ways that allow them to achieve results that were once inconceivable".

I like International NLP Trainer Charles Faulkner's definition of NLP in "The New Market Wizards" a book about excellent Traders. He says:

"NLP studies great achievers to pinpoint their mental programs – that is, to learn how great achievers use their brains to produce results. The models of the natural learning processes these people used to become extraordinary in their fields can be used by anyone wishing to excel."

Charles lists six key steps in achievement:

1. Use both toward and away from motivation. (More about this later).

2. Have a goal of full capability plus, with anything less being unacceptable.

3. Break down potentially overwhelming goals into chunks, with satisfaction garnered from the completion of each individual step.

4. Fully concentrate on the present moment of time – that is, the single task at hand rather than the long-term goal.

5. Personally involve yourself in achieving goals (as opposed to depending on others)

6. Make self-to-self comparisons to measure progress.

Here's another definition from Sue Knight who is an international consultant and author pioneering the use of NLP in leadership in business.

> "NLP is the process of modelling (studying) the structure of subjective experience, which means that in NLP we assume that there is a structure to the way that we do things. This structure consists of patterns of thoughts and behaviours that make up strategies, and so on this basis we

can assume that we each have our own unique strategies for how we make decisions, how we learn, how we build relationships, how we negotiate, how we get up in the morning, how we get ourselves stressed.

Whatever we do we have a strategy for how we do it. Most of the elements and usually the key pieces are out of our conscious awareness. So if I admire something that you do – for example the way in which you build instant rapport with complete strangers – and if I were to ask you how you do that, what you tell me would be useless to me because far from being what you actually do you would just tell me what you think you do.

The application of NLP to business is to model what we perceive to be excellent in any context – for example top presenters, successful salespeople in specific contexts, in order to reproduce the results that they get, either for ourselves or to give back to them (to get greater consistency in their results) or to train others.

Since the term NLP was developed by John Grinder and Richard Bandler, there have been thousands and thousands of modelling projects. These modelling projects uncovered patterns of thinking, patterns in language and patterns in behaviour that makes the difference in the context of the study. Amongst the earliest discoveries were predicates and eye accessing cues (see Appendices, page 280/81). They are examples of the output of NLP – they are not NLP.

> NLP is about finding out for yourself what works and what can work for you by modelling other people or yourself in situations where they or you are getting the results that you want to reproduce."

– Sue Knight, international consultant and author pioneering the use of NLP in leadership in business.

From an NLP point of view we want to know what the person is doing on the outside such as their behaviours and the skills they bring to those activities as well as what they are doing on the inside in their thinking? What are they seeing, hearing, and feeling on the inside and in what sequence, how are they motivating themselves and what beliefs do they have in this context?

So modelling someone being excellent is not only about learning about what they are doing but also learning **how** to learn to really understand **how** a person is able to consistently perform in an excellent way and then be able to take on those skills ourselves, streamlining them so only what is essential is used and the test is always, does it work for us and can we teach it to others?

"Make things as simple as possible but no simpler" – Albert Einstein

NLP is not about theory its about what works.

There were definitely some "ah ha" moments for me during and after my first experience of NLP Training and I realised that there is a way to understand human behaviour and rearrange the "building blocks" of the structure of thinking to take care of problems, transform those feelings that always held me back; that is to say change my own programming that then changes my perception of what is possible for me and I am able to see different pictures of my own future in my mind without the constant fear of failure and be able to build more successful futures.

Aikido is the process of discovering the pathways of no resistance and learning how to manipulate the hips and angles and gain power from pushing out of the ground.

NLP is delving into our own or in the case of coaching, someone else's mind for the purpose of solving problems and finding and/or building new pathways in the brain. Pretty much the same thing, I think.

NLP does not operate out of a problem frame but rather an outcome frame. There is a basic NLP model for change that does require that we find out what the current situation is, what's stopping you from achieving your goal, how come you haven't yet achieved it and then what resources are required to get you to the desired state and how to access those resources now. What we don't do is delve after more and more information about the problem.

NLP, whatever way you look at it, is about solving people's problems by knowing how to find out how to create choices and operate in a different way, firstly to know how to manage your own state, know what you want, clarify those wants or goals and know how to make the necessary adjustments in your behaviour and take the appropriate steps that will enable you to successfully achieve your goals.

Present State ⟶ Resources ⟶ Desired State

Once you have a goal you have a problem, i.e. how to achieve it and if you are stuck then there are two useful questions you can ask:

- What's stopping you?
- What do you want instead?

The second question will elicit another outcome so you can loop around and ask the questions again and again, chunking down until you get to a point where you can see yourself take some action, now or at least in the next 5 minutes.

Lets go through an example of this simple but powerful process that is called "Stepping Down".

The goal in this example is:

I want to finish this book

What's stopping you?

I keep getting ideas for more material

What do you want instead?

I want to know how to decide its finished

What's stopping you?

I don't have any previous experience of being in this position

What do you want instead?

A way of assessing if there is enough information

What's stopping you?

I don't have that experience and ability

What do you want instead?

Find someone who has previous experience of writing a book and ask him or her "how do you know when the book is finished? What's your evidence?

What's stopping you?

Nothing, I know someone who has done that and I will ask them if they are willing to read the book and assess whether, in their opinion, it is finished or maybe needs a bit more. I think now I will know when its finished when it feels finished.

In any activity the starting point is to know what you want and in regard to modelling the key NLP question is **"How do you do that?"** This sense of curiosity is a prerequisite for learning.

There is a NLP model called "Neurological Levels" which is an adaption by Robert Dilts of Gregory Bateson's notion of "Logical Levels", which helps to explain, unpack and discover what is going on for anyone at all levels.

NEURO-LOGICAL LEVELS

Spirituality – Your place and relationship to Nature. For a business it means how the business connects with the community and other organisations.
Awakener

Identity – Who? Mission. A sense of yourself and organisational identity is the business culture. It emerges from the interaction of the other levels.
Sponsor

Beliefs & Values – Why? Permission. Motivation. Beliefs are the principles that guide actions. They are filters and rules. Businesses have principles they act on and values they hold. Beliefs and values direct our lives, acting both as prohibitions and permissions on how we act.
Mentor

Capabilities – How? Mental strategies that guide actions and reactions, maps and skills people develop to guide their specific behaviours. Business processes and procedures.
Teacher

Behaviours – What? These are the actions, reactions and thoughts through which we interact with people and the environment around us. What we do. Seen from the outside.
Coach

Environment – Where? When? Charles Faulkner calls this "Psycho-geography". Context/Constraints. You set the boundary on what to include. You may be successful only in specific circumstances or with particular people. "Being in the right place at the right time."
Guide

Robert Dilts says: *"This model was developed to describe the different levels of learning and change in human beings and human systems. Each level organises and directs the interactions on the level below it like a hierarchy of influence and relationship."*

It's useful both as a diagnostic map for problem solving and also for creating personal and organisational alignment. One way to do this is to consider your issue or outcome from each one of these levels.

It's important to not only consider the "issue" or "outcome" from these different levels but also to actually do that by standing in the space of each level. This way we are engaging the whole system of mind and body, neurology and physiology and are associated in the "issue" so we are experiencing the situation in the present and we will get a feeling that lets us know whether everything is balanced and congruent or not at each level.

When you are sitting down or standing back and looking at yourself doing this you would be disassociated and not experiencing the situation but watching it and yourself from the outside which will get you different information. Both are of value.

As you stand in each level you are asking yourself: Are you capable of doing this and do you believe it is possible and OK for you to be this person and identifying at which level you may not be congruent and then working at making adjustments needed to incorporate the necessary changes and resources. So for instance you may discover that you don't believe you can do this and you may then go off and get some training and this will change that belief.

The skills and approaches for coaching, leadership and influence are different at each level. In education and life there is often confusion between the levels of Identity and behaviour. We are not what we do. People who smoke cigarettes, which is behaviour, something they are doing, often refer to themselves as "smokers" which is an identity level label, who they are.

Children are often labelled in school, at the level of identity, as poor learners or a bad or stupid person rather than getting feedback on what they are doing. This is a good way to create phobias around learning and limiting beliefs about themselves. I think that as well as "learning disabilities" we could say there are also "teaching disabilities".

As Mark Twain once said: *"Education can get in the way of learning".*

It is much easier to change something at the levels of behaviour and capability, something you are doing, rather than identity, which is about who you are.

You are not what you do?

"Our life is the creation of our mind." – Buddha

From the point of view of modelling it is useful to understand what is going on at all of these levels for the exemplar, the person with the skill, and what we are looking for as a modeller is "the difference that makes the difference" and this will often be unconscious to the person performing the skill.

As Sue Knight said in her definition of NLP Modelling:

"If I were to ask you how you do that, what you tell me would be useless to me because far from being what you actually do you would just tell me what you think you do."

Gregory Bateson said: *"Difference is the difference that makes the difference".*

The exemplar may tell you what they think they are doing which is known as teaching and the modeller will also be able to discover that which is performed out of their conscious awareness. An example of this is when people say they just got a feeling but feelings don't usually happen on their own. They are generally driven or created by an internal picture such as a memory or a visualisation of a future scenario, a sound or smell and taste that then evokes or triggers the feeling associated with those thoughts.

The piece that the person is consciously aware of is the feeling and the internal picture, sound or smell is happening, very fast, just out of your conscious awareness. Knowing this you can back up and put your conscious attention on what's happening just before the feeling until you can bring the internal picture, sound, smell or taste to your conscious awareness.

If it's a positive feeling you can continue to increase the intensity by enlarging the picture, bringing it closer and turning up the colour. If it's a negative feeling we know what to do to stop it; change the internal picture by shrinking it in size, turning down the brightness and sound and sending it off over the horizon.

When you change your thinking you will change how you feel and what actions you take.

"Until you make the unconscious conscious, it will direct your life and you will call it fate" – Carl Jung

A NLP modeller would be able to detect that there is something else happening out of the person's conscious awareness and ask them about it. Some of the "out of awareness" indicators would be eye movements (see Appendices, page 280/81), physiology, gestures, language and submodalities such as tone of voice.

Submodalities are the qualities of our internal representations such as big or small internal pictures, volume of internal sounds and location of internal feelings.

INTERRUPTION

I was suddenly stopped from writing these notes when the hard drive on my computer broke and I lost all of my files along with thousands of photographs. Despite paying a company to recover the data they said they were unable to get any information back. So I let go of the book because I couldn't face attempting to write it all again.

But then I remembered I had given a hard copy to a Romanian guy I had met on a NLP Master Practitioner course I was coaching on and I sent an email to him in Romania asking him if he would send me a copy of my notes.

Three months went by and I never heard from him so I thought we had lost contact and once again gave up the project. Then surprisingly he responded, (thanks Sorel), and sent me copies of about 15 pages of material I had written. He had scanned each one and they arrived as jpeg files, which I couldn't work on, as they weren't text files. I now realise I could have probably used software from the web to convert them to text files but at that time thought I had to retype each one of the pages.

I started typing, slowly, but gradually lost my motivation leaving ten pages untyped. After all why was I bothering? It wasn't going to be published. But along came eBooks and Kindle and I was then re-motivated to complete the typing and finish the piece as it was now possible to publish on Kindle and I could see a finished article that felt worth working towards.

Somehow I needed to get it out of my system and off my timeline and I think the process of putting all this information together was really about my own learning and my own journey.

It can make you feel good to go to that place in time in your mind as if you had already achieved your goal and look back to see what it was that you did to achieve it. My project then seemed to take on a life of its own; I continually noticed examples of these principles in my NLP work and while training in Aikido. The project refused to lie dormant and I am now happy and excited to be able to share it with you.

In this essay I propose to set out the strategies that transcend conflict and show you how you can use these principles to succeed in your own life, just like the old man did on the train in Terry Dobson's story at the beginning.

How did he manage to get the raging drunk's attention in a non-threatening way and have a conversation with him? Isn't that what we all want to be able to do, yes.

During Aikido training when you are held strongly by someone, despite the automatic response of tension and struggle to get free, like Terry Dobson's thoughts about fighting the drunken man, there is a way around their strength and anger but initially our response is to use our strength and fight against that grip.

We have to retrain ourselves out of that "automatic" response of struggle and use of strength and employ new ways of reacting. We are wiring in a new program and your job then is to find the way around that strength and power, and utilise the pathway of no resistance, so you can bypass the block, both mental and physical, with ease.

Recently I was training with a very strong guy and I was aware of that and as I felt his grip tighten on my wrist I unconsciously became strong myself by tensing up and got a bit stuck during the exercise. Next time I made sure I was doing all the basics correctly and although this did make a difference it was still a bit of a struggle.

I thought about this all week and remembered that the Sensei had been emphasising how to respond to strength with softness and the first thing to do was to relax the shoulder, my shoulder that is. So the next time I trained with the same guy I made a point of being soft and relaxing my shoulder and to my amazement, even though he was still holding me strongly, all of his strength disappeared and I was able to complete the technique without any struggle.

Aikido is full of paradoxes and this is one here. When someone holds you strongly, rather than responding with strength, fighting and struggling against it, relax and let him or her have the grip and move the rest of your body that is not being held. They only have hold of you in one place and therefore you can let them have the grip and move your body off the center line where they could strike or kick you and from that angle, where they are weakened, you can get around their point of strength and power.

You can change the angle that you move to a place where they can no longer resist such as to their side and the stronger they hold you the more they will be moved off balance when you find that pathway and redirect and capture the energy created by their resistance. Often you can lower yourself a little so when you move you don't bang into the grip and avoid the point where you are held and the ability to make that movement is, as Saito Sensei said, all in the hips and the angles.

CHAPTER 2 – AIKIDO

"Military tactics are like water. For water, in its natural course, runs away from high places and hastens downwards. So, in war, the way is to avoid what is strong and strike at what is weak."
– Miyamoto Musashi

I remember the first time I saw Akira Kurosawa's film "Seven Samurai" in about 1969 at The Brighton Film Centre (sadly now long gone), and after seeing the sword fight, asking myself: "How did he do that?" This was the fight where the master swordsman, Kyuzo, (played by Seiji Miayaguchi) kills his opponent with a single stroke, having reluctantly accepted the challenge to duel.

My immediate reaction to seeing this dramatic scene was to ask myself, sitting there in the dark of the cinema, the question:

"How did he do that?"

That is the NLP modelling question, as you will remember, although this was long before I ever discovered NLP and in fact it wasn't yet a formed discipline at that time.

Many years later in the early 1980s I was inspired to start Aikido training after seeing a bit of film of an elderly man dealing with continuous attacks from several people. It got my attention immediately and I was very curious about how he was moving. It looked and felt that there was no clash of strength and what he was doing appeared effortless.

In that moment I knew that I wanted to find out more about this Martial Art, which I later learned, was called Aikido and so I started to train, firstly once a week at an Adult Education Centre in the City of London with Karl Lancaster Sensei. I trained with Karl for a few years and then with Andy Hathaway Sensei at The London Aikido Club where there are classes every day.

I had always been interested in learning a martial art but Karate was the only one I was aware of and it had never appealed to me. I had done some boxing at school and was OK but there was always kids who were bigger, faster and stronger both inside and outside school.

I also played rugby and football so at least I had ball skills, speed and balance and evasion techniques.

Many years later when I saw Aikido being done I realised that there was a way to deal with strength and size without having to be bigger and stronger myself. Later I was to discover that the skills and principles used in Aikido could be applied in life generally.

About 5 years ago I was asked to speak to a group who were starting on a NLP Master Practitioner course, about my work. I presented the usual verbal profile of being a NLP Coach and Trainer and whilst enlarging on this found myself talking about learning and learning how to learn.

I reminded the group that the whole field of NLP came from having a sense of curiosity and fascination about what people are doing in order to be effective. It wasn't that they had a god-given talent but rather that they were employing certain strategies in their thinking that determines their internal state and their actions, in order to succeed. These strategies can be modelled, learnt, used by our selves and taught to others - the study of excellence. This is the essence of NLP.

I went on to explain to the group that I thought my interest in NLP probably came from my father. He was from a poor background in rural Southern Ireland and he and his brothers learnt to be self-reliant. They had to be able to build and mend things and if they didn't have the tools they would have to make their own. Out of scarcity and adversity came resourcefulness and many skills so there was always the curiosity and fascination in how something worked so they could learn to do it themselves if necessary. Sometimes it was the only choice.

As a kid I spent many hours in the evenings holding the lamp while my father hunched over his car engine. This was boring for me but later paid off when I needed my motorbike mending. To my surprise I had unconsciously learnt and absorbed many things about engines while standing there holding the lamp. In NLP this unconscious uptake of information is known as implicit modelling.

We cannot not learn and this is how we learn so fast as babies, absorbing information from around us, partly as a necessity to be able to function and survive and also to be able to know how to be successful in our lives. Basically, knowing how to achieve our outcomes (goals).

Time gives us the ability to take "the longer view", a different perspective and looking back now, through time, I can see a whole series of cause/effects connecting back to my childhood. It was only when I was telling all of this to the group that I realised that my own sense of curiosity had been unconsciously modelled from my father and his quest to find out "how" so he could do it himself. For him it was about economics and survival, for me it became curiosity about the process and to ask, "How do you do that?"

There is a tradition of recording "The Way of the Warrior" so that you can transfer the principles and strategies employed successfully on the battlefield and use them to succeed in other areas of your life such as business, sports, relationships, negotiations, health, creativity, personal development and even world affairs.

Sun Tzu's book "The Art of War" and Miyamoto Musashi's "The Book of Five Rings" is two examples of this genre. Sun Tzu said he preferred to win without fighting or, at the very least, to win the easiest battles first.

"Military tactics are like water. For water, in its natural course, runs away from high places and hastens downwards. So, in war, the way is to avoid what is strong and strike at what is weak."

Aikido founder, Morihei Ueshiba's writings, his many quotes, poems and sayings heard by others are recorded in "The Art of Peace" which is also the meaning of the word Aikido although this is mostly translated as "The Way of Harmony".

Morihei Ueshiba, known as O Sensei, also recorded 50 of his techniques in a book entitled "Budo" and his writings have been published in conjunction with contemporary translators.

The many sayings and quotes attributed to O-Sensei in the "Art of Peace" may have been translated and edited with a bias to "fit in" with contemporary western thinking and as a way of popularising Aikido throughout the world and some of his language was difficult to put into English and many Japanese Sensei who trained with him at that time had different ideas about what he was saying.

Stanley Pranin, the late editor of Aikido Journal, has researched and written a lot about this and working with three native Japanese speakers, attempted to get some of O Sensei's recorded passages translated. None of these three translators could agree on what the contemporary meaning was and their attempt was eventually abandoned.

Also, at that time, there was the prohibition of any martial art in Japan imposed by the Americans directly after the war, so care was needed in describing Aikido.

However I think the book "The Art of Peace" is a way we can get some understanding of O Sensei's thinking.

Morihiro Saito Shihan said in an interview with Aikido Journal that in true budo, you do not express yourself in words or writing.

"God does not give grace to those who talk too much. This is what O'Sensei said and a philosophical perspective is also important. When O'Sensei started to talk about aikido, it became tales about God".

So I hope that I am not talking too much and I trust that these two great Masters would have approved of my attempt to explore in words these universal principles of excellence.

MAPPING ACROSS

From my early training days onward many NLP Trainers would refer to Aikido and its ideas on non-conflict. Later on I discovered that John Grinder who, along with Richard Bandler founded the field of NLP, had been in the United States Army Special Forces, known as the Green Berets and was also in a US Intelligence Agency and being a multi-linguist as well as a man of action, was parachuted into East Germany during the period of the "cold war" to help Defectors reach the West safely. He may have trained in Aikido and subsequently recommended it to his NLP students.

The word "Aikido" is formed of three kanji:

- 合 – ai – joining, unifying, combining, fit
- 気 – ki – spirit, energy, breath, morale
- 道 – dō – way, path

Aikido is known for its revolutionary principles of non-conflict and caused quite a stir in the conservative world of the martial arts in Japan in the 20th century. According to O Sensei:

"The martial arts are not about victory over others but victory over our selves."

My outcome is to present these ancient winning strategies and principles and the ideas of the process of non-conflict, as developed by O Sensei and carefully preserved and codified by Saito Shihan, and show how they can be applied, alongside the contemporary field of NLP.

I started Aikido training in 1984 and NLP training in 1990 and soon realised that there are a lot of similarities between the two disciplines and that their core principles are the same. Musashi and O Sensei's techniques were tried and tested in combat so only what worked was passed on. They were continually modelling the minutiae of excellent martial skills as well as psychological strategies and techniques.

NLP is the study of the structure of subjective experience and the field comes from the modelling of excellence, what works consistently, with all redundancy streamlined out, so it is not surprising that the martial principles which a Samurai warrior or contemporary Aikidoka studies and employs to succeed, survive and flourish, are the same as those discovered from NLP modelling. Both NLP and Aikido are studying excellence, what is useful and what consistently works.

The aim of this book is to present some of the principles of NLP and Aikido and show how they are intertwined and are in fact universal principles for success in any context.

So as I asked earlier, what is important to you now about having these universal principles that you can follow easily and for what purpose do you want them?

I wanted these skills and I guess some of you reading this book want these skills as well, yes.

Morihei Ueshiba (1883 – 1969), known in the Aikido world as O Sensei (Master or Great Teacher), was born into a Samurai family in Wakayama Prefecture in Japan.

Samurai is the term for the military nobility of pre-industrial Japan. An early reference to the word "Samurai" appears in the Kokin Wakashū (905–914), the first imperial anthology of poems, completed in the first part of the 10th century.

By the end of the 12th century, Samurai became almost entirely synonymous with bushi and the word was closely associated with the middle and upper echelons of the warrior class. The samurai followed a set of rules that came to be known as bushido (Way of the Warrior) and similar to the concept of chivalry.

The Samurai code of ethics consisted of:

- patience
- frugality
- constant self-improvement, now known in western business as kaizen

Kaizen is the practice of continuous improvement and was originally introduced to the West by Masaaki Imai in his 1986 book "Kaizen: The Key to Japan's Competitive Success". Today kaizen is recognized worldwide as an important pillar of an organization's long-term competitive strategy.

While they numbered less than 10% of Japan's population, Samurai teachings can still be found today in both everyday life and in modern Japanese martial arts.

A Samurai warrior was highly trained and skilled in the use of many weapons as well as being trained in more "right brain" activities or other arts such as Sumi-e painting, Haiku, (poetry) and Ikebana, (flower arranging). On horseback and in armour he was a formidable fighter and the aim of his opponents was to unhorse him by an arrow shot either to the horse or the warrior, if they could penetrate his armour, so the foot soldiers could then deal with him on the ground.

However a Samurai warrior was equally dangerous on foot and bristled with weapons so foot soldiers would immediately grab him to prevent him using his swords. Two or more soldiers would hold him while another one would finish him off, usually with a spear thrust. It was therefore essential that a Samurai warrior had ways of dealing with multiple attackers and if he was being held he had the physical knowledge and ability to get around the attackers' strength and power, draw his sword and escape, win or both. There are Aikido techniques that come directly from how a warrior draws his sword while his hands and arm are being held.

Struggling against 3 or more opponents is probably not going to work so they had to learn ways to deal with overwhelming physical odds by understanding and using the laws of physics and be, as O Sensei said: "In harmony with the Universe" and this is where the idea of non-conflict in Aikido comes in.

The martial art schools in Japan in the early 20th Century were often owned and run by families with their own techniques and styles, which were mostly kept secret from others.

O Sensei travelled Japan in search of some of these exceptional teachers in the martial arts, managed to train with them and became skilled in many systems and on occasions had to test those skills in combat. He became an accomplished and renowned swordsman and after many years of training and combat he began to develop and teach Aikido after adapting his techniques to go around, blend with and utilise an opponent's strength and momentum so that you can deal with a number of attackers at the same time.

The following is a quote from Wikipedia and the many historical books about Aikido:

The real birth of Aikido came as the result of three instances of spiritual awakening that Morihei Ueshiba (O Sensei) experienced. The first happened in 1925, after Ueshiba had defeated a Naval Officer's bokken (wooden sword) attacks unarmed and without hurting the officer. O Sensei then walked to his garden and experienced a "spiritual awakening".

"I felt the universe suddenly quake, and that a golden spirit sprang up from the ground, veiled my body, and changed my body into a golden one. At the same time my body became light. I was able to understand the whispering of the birds, and was clearly aware of the mind of God, the creator of the universe."

At that moment I was enlightened: the source of Budo is God's love - the spirit of loving protection for all beings... Budo is not the felling of an opponent by force; nor is it a tool to lead the world to destruction with arms. True Budo is to accept the spirit of the universe, keep the peace of the world, correctly produce, protect and cultivate all beings in nature."

Converting an attacker to a follower is like the NLP definition of leadership:

"Building a community that other people want to belong to."

People are drawn or are led into the "community": they feel that as a result of their communications, verbal and physical, they have a desire to be there. Whenever I see films of O Sensei it looks and I feel that he is training with a sense of joy. There is an energy and bounce in him and his movements and even-though he "defeats" the Naval Officer he does it with and perhaps because of this "sense of joy", (my hallucination). He has amazing timing and is always in control, initiating the attacks.

I have experienced this a lot in training where and when a piece of coaching is given with a sense of it being a gift on the journey and is another piece to improve the technique. It is an amazing feeling.

Budo is a Japanese term describing modern Japanese Martial Arts. According to western translators it means the "Martial Way", and may be thought of as the "Way of War" or "Way of Combat".

However, the oriental concept is actually much different from the western concept. The character "bu" is constructed from the characters meaning "arms of war" or "violence," and "to stop, prohibit, or bring to an end." Therefore, "bu" is more accurately translated as "to stop violence", a moving away strategy or "to bring about peace", a moving towards strategy and perhaps using both strategies gives us leverage.

This idea of leverage occurs in some Aikido techniques where the opponent's body is moved from two different positions, pulling one way and pushing the other, like a capstan.

The warriors of China and Japan saw their skills as tools for maintaining the peace rather than indulgences in a love of war. And although warfare was sometimes necessary to restore peace, peace was always the ultimate goal.

O Sensei's "Spiritual Awakening" was clearly what is known in NLP and Hypnosis as an "altered state" and from this state O Sensei experienced revelations and moments of "enlightenment". He also studied the Oomoto religion of Onisaburo Deguchi for a period of 8 years, a believer in the Oomoto maxim that it was humanity's duty to move forward together, bringing about a new age of existence on Earth.

His second experience occurred in 1940 when:

"Around 2am as I was performing misogi, (practice of ritual purification) I suddenly forgot all the martial techniques I had ever learned. The techniques of my teachers appeared completely new. Now they were vehicles for the cultivation of life, knowledge, and virtue, not just devices to throw people with."

From the special state he would have been in from doing Misogi he was able to get a change of perspective or a reframing of the meaning of the Martial Arts.

His third experience was in 1942 during the worst fighting of WWII, O Sensei had a vision of the "Great Spirit of Peace".

This is not an Aikido history book and that would be a very interesting project for another time and perhaps for another person, however, Aikido is not the only art with a higher moral compass. Other arts have, for hundreds of years, professed the same or similar goals and ethics.

Does it matter? No, it's like NLP Modelling, O Sensei studied and took the best so he was also the inheritor of a technical and philosophical tradition as well as being Aikido's originator.

At about this time and in his 50s he went to live in the then small town of Iwama about 100km north east of Tokyo, where he had previously purchased land and started farming, doing his paintings and continuing to practise and teach his arts. Iwama is now known as the home of Aikido and is where the Aiki shrine was built.

These events had a profound effect on O Sensei and it is widely believed led to him adapting the techniques he had learnt, to create the art of Aikido. He said:

"The Way of the Warrior has been misunderstood. It is not a means to kill and destroy others. Those who seek to compete and better one another are making a terrible mistake. To smash, injure, or destroy is the worst thing a human being can do. The real Way of a Warrior is to prevent such slaughter - it is the Art of Peace, the power of love."

O Sensei talked about being in harmony with the Universe. I have been told about and have seen pictures taken from spacecraft, satellites and the Hubble

Telescope that clearly show that our Galaxy is a vast spiral shape and Aikido matches and utilises this spiral shape, this pathway of energy.

When we are able to match an opponent's movement and take their balance well enough, we can then lead them and return their energy along the pathway of a spiral, avoiding any conflict, no collision, a natural pathway of continuous connection and as Andy Hathaway Sensei often says it is like landing a fish. It is important to maintain your connection by keeping the line taught.

An opponent's strength is bypassed and any resistance provides energy, which can be used by matching its direction and the opponent is then led along the edge of that spiral. A circle would mean that you would return to where the energy came from, causing a collision and thus conflict.

The Communication Loop

It is the matching, both physical and mental, that is at the heart of non-conflict and enables another person to be influenced in a physical way because, instead of fighting against the attack, we blend with it, match its direction and energy; therefore there is no resistance. This also opens up the possibility to influence people in other ways. How we lead the person will also affect other possible attackers by closing down their options or offering them openings that are really bait.

"Hold out baits to entice the enemy" – Sun Tzu, The Art of War

Communication is the most desired soft skill.

We cannot not communicate and therefore we cannot not have an influence. Even if we are not speaking our very presence will have an effect.

These spirals can be large flowing movements or small and tight like a screw, turning around and moving forward at the same time and the the whole body moves, pushing from the ground, legs straightening and hips turning up through the torso and projecting energy, known as kokyu, along this spiral pathway and out through the fingers. This has to be coordinated with the "attack" of the other person so they are caught up in this spiral. These movements are powerful because a spiral doesn't experience "resistance" and ultimately matches the spiral shape of the Galaxy and thus we are, as O Sensei said, in harmony with the Universe.

Every Aikido class ends with Kokyu Ho. I can't really explain what kokyu is. I can tell you a few things about it but you would really have to do it to learn it. You need to feel it.

According to the Japanese the word "Kokyu" has four main meanings, the first of which is "breath" and it can also mean "an art or knack", "the gist of something" or a "rhythm, tone or tune" and it may also suggest a "sense of harmony".

I once asked Paolo Corralini Shihan what he thought the equivalent of Kokyu is in life and he replied that it was the utilisation of everything that is available to us wherever we are and with whatever we are doing in that moment.

My revelation is that the equivalent to kokyu is mindfulness.

It reminds me of what Isadora Duncan, the pioneer of modern dance, said when she was asked about a dance.

"If I could tell you what it meant, there would be no point in dancing it" – Isadora Duncan

This is a photograph of the blackboard in the London Aikido Club with some notes made by Andy Hathaway Sensei for instructors and students.

He writes on the dojo blackboard:

"From DNA to Hurricanes"

From micro to macro, everything is connected.

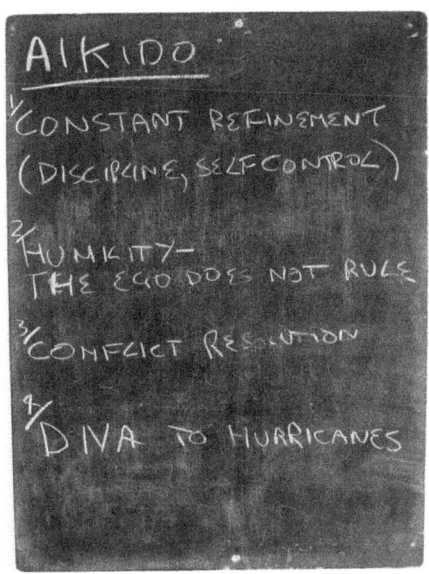

No. 4 refers to the spirals that exist in all aspects of our world including our own bodies. Examples of this can be seen in Leonardo Da Vinci's stunning anatomical drawings made 500 years ago.

"The Art of Peace is the principle of non-resistance. Because it is non-resistant it is victorious from the beginning. Those with evil intentions or contentious thoughts are vanquished. The Art of Peace is invincible because it contends with nothing." O Sensei.

Another great swordsman, Miyamoto Musashi, who lived in the 16th and early 17th century, after a lifetime serving different Lords and undefeated in many swordfights, starting at the age of 13, also retreated for a long period and came to realise that the principles he had learnt to fight with were transferable and could be applied in many other ways as well. Instead of an opponent in a sword fight it could be a business meeting, a negotiation, a relationship or an army of 10,000. The context and content may change but the principles and the processes are the same and enable the achievement of excellence and success.

Musashi also sculpted in wood and metal, was a calligrapher and made Sumi-e paintings, which are an expression of Zen, using a brush and ink to illustrate scenes of nature, right brain activities that help integration of both brain hemispheres and enable ways to access other resources, a balancing of the entire system, yin and yang.

The practice of developing other skills and activities also applies to contemporary successful people be they warriors or those who succeed in any other field. These are also the archetypical energies of warrior, lover and joker that bring in more strength, softness and playfulness.

"We stand with one foot either side of the corpus callosum" – Judith Delozier (co-developer in the field of NLP)

Musashi wrote down his thoughts and teachings, and they are available in "The Book of Five Rings" and he and O Sensei, despite being four centuries apart in time, both went through a period of reflection and search for perfection of technique and studied other disciplines to broaden their knowledge.

"The way to be more confident is to be more competent." – Richard Bandler, co-founder of NLP

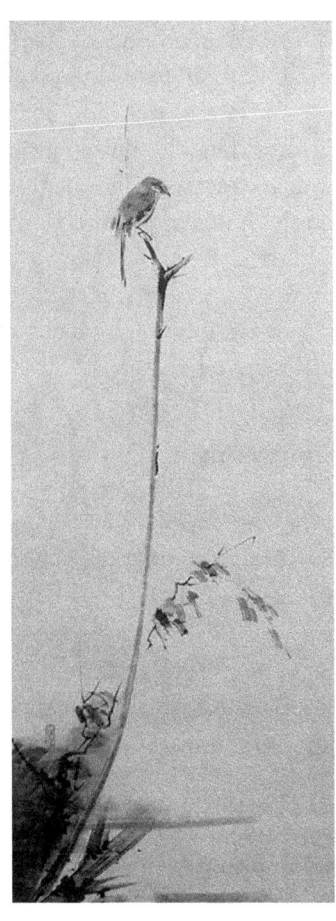

Musashi is well known for his paintings of birds, such as "Koboku Meikakuzu" (Shrike on a Dead Tree).

English Mountaineer, Joe Simpson said:

"Rock climbing is frightening but I found out if you knew what you're doing you could get rid of the fear."

When O Sensei experienced the event, which he later described as being bathed in golden light, and during which he had a realisation that the martial arts had a greater purpose other than the destruction of people and that they are about harmony as in nature, and are for the benefit of all people, he then set about refining his skills to this aim and started to create the art of Aikido, the way of harmony, and travelled and taught throughout Japan. His long-term students became instructors and some of them introduced Aikido to many areas of the world where it flourishes today.

O Sensei drew on his many skills learnt over a 20-year period from the great Takeda Sensei who taught the art of Daito Ryu Aiki Jujitsu. O Sensei was a master of Kenjutsu, the art of the sword and developed and taught a brilliant and sophisticated empty handed fighting system based on the laws of nature, harmony, balance as well as Budo (fighting spirit) and encouraged people to learn these principles by studying Aikido, a physical metaphor bringing the idea of non-conflict into their lives in many other ways.

In my experience Aikido practitioners do not get into fights. Experiencing doing and receiving Aikido helps us realise that there are other ways to deal with conflict. We learn to train in such a way that we don't give openings and we look for the openings that an opponent may give and when our balance is taken and a technique is applied correctly we let go and take the fall. Either that or we are in danger of getting injured. You can't really cut loose in Aikido.

The most conflict you will ever have is going to be within yourself. So accept the gift of feedback and train to deal with yourself.

The aim of Aikido is to blend with the strength, energy and momentum of the attacker, which is called "Awase", and then, either redirect the force of their attack rather than opposing it head on, enter to their rear, the principle of irimi, or go around their strength. This requires less reliance on physical strength and power comes from Awase, capturing the balance and delivering atemi, strikes to vital points.

Aikido is not a get fit system; when you train consistently you will get fitter but it is a far more sophisticated Budo and self-development system than just for fitness just as Hypnosis is much more than a set of tools for tricks.

An aikidoka (aikido student) blends with and leads the attackers' momentum as well as using entering and turning movements. All of the techniques also include strikes (atemi) to vital points that can stop someone and are completed with various locks, holds and throws. The aim is to put your partner in a position whereby, as a result of your own body movement, they can't avoid falling. The ability to do this is contained in awase and correct use of the basics that are the "set up" and facilitate the techniques, all of which require taking the other persons balance in some way.

The Aikido strategy of "getting off the line of attack" creates a safe space within conflict. This feeling of safety allows one to be more completely present in Aikido and by using the same principles of blending the same applies to therapy or coaching or any other human interaction. By blending with the attack and moving off line at the same time means there is nothing there to fight against and the opponent, training partner or client can be taken off-balance and led forward towards some sort of conclusion.

As O Sensei said:

"I am always victorious as I contend with nothing."

Realising that "Getting off the line" and experiencing the attacker moving through without hurting the practitioner can be a transformative experience for Aikidoka and NLP Coaches alike and are ways to change yourself rather than the outer world.

Aikido is not a self-defence system. There is no defence and then attack. Your defence is your attack so that the first thing you do must give you the edge and even better is to anticipate the intention of attack and smother it by initiating your own attack or your own intention, and this can be demonstrated in how you present yourself so the other person, seeing and realising this, may think twice about doing anything. Sometimes the wisest thing to do is stand your ground, take stock, move in, withdraw or not be there. If you see a group of drunken football supporters coming towards you, it will be useful to cross the road.

In any encounter, martial or otherwise, we are aiming to connect with the other person and be so engaged that you can respond to the smallest of movement.

Josh Waitzkin, a chess grand master and world Tai Chi Chuan Push Hands Champion talks about when an opponent pushes he withdraws, the opponent pushes again and he withdraws so a pattern is being set up and he has sort of trained his opponent to continue the pattern and the next time he pushes Josh responds differently and takes his balance. Of course this all happens in seconds or less whereby there isn't time for conscious thought and you depend on all that training, the 10,000 hours, so the physical skills are wired in and you can respond automatically.

"Knowledge is only rumour until it is in the muscle" – New Guinea Proverb

This is the same as when we are working or talking with someone else, we are in a communication loop, an on-going feedback system where we are connected. We see, hear and feel what the other person is saying and doing by keeping our selves present and being mindful. As long as we can build and maintain a connection and be in rapport we will have an influence on the other person and of course we will also be open to being influenced as well because we are also in the same loop. When a person is having difficulty with someone in a relationship they often blame the other person and forget about their part in the system and their expectation is for the other side to change in some way. Maybe that might work but usually it causes an impasse.

When you watch film clips of O Sensei they clearly show, despite offering his wrist to be grabbed, how he always took the initiative and delivered almost imperceptible atemi (strikes) either before or during techniques that momentarily surprised and stopped the opponent from delivering a proper full-hearted attack.

"The highest level of swordsmanship is said to be "swordless" technique, evading rather than striking and this is like the art that O Sensei developed whereby in a duel what was accomplished was the transformation of an enemy, via his way of fighting, into a great and loyal friend. This is part of the essential message of aikido and what O Sensei was trying to teach". – Aikido Journal

CHAPTER 3 – LEARN LIKE A BABY

Confusion is not a state of not knowing but rather new information that you have not yet organised.

John Grinder, an assistant professor in the linguistics faculty of the University of California in Santa Cruz, and Richard Bandler, a mathematician, computer scientist and psychology student at the same university, began to develop NLP in the early 1970s.

NLP stands for neuro linguistic programming and refers to the connection between neurological processes, language and behavioural patterns that have been learned through experience.

Bandler and Grinder were both interested in how people change and they observed various therapists in action with individuals and groups, most of whom they found to be unsuccessful in what they were claiming to do and the ones who were successful were mostly unable to explain what they were doing and therefore not able to teach it to others.

They discovered two therapists who were consistently successful in what they were doing with their clients and began by modelling them. They were Virginia Satir who pioneered family therapy and Fritz Perls who was the founder of Gestalt Therapy.

Bandler and Grinders' friend Gregory Bateson, a British anthropologist and writer, referred them to Milton

Erickson who was a Psychiatrist, Psychologist and Hypnotherapist specialising in medical hypnosis and family therapy. Bateson said Erickson was consistently excellent and successful in his work and many therapists would send or take their "difficult" clients to visit him in Phoenix.

Erickson said that he worked with people in a way that enabled them to discover and utilise their own resources, which they already had and had not been fully aware of until then and utilisation means going with the flow, as in Aikido.

A teenage boy finds his burly father desperately trying – and failing – to push a reluctant cow into their barn. The young lad, weak from a recent bout of polio, comes up behind the recalcitrant cow and firmly tugs on its tail. The cow immediately heads in the opposite direction…into the barn. Problem solved.

That farm boy was Milton Erickson, arguably the greatest psychotherapist and hypnotherapist in history. He never founded a school of therapy and many of his therapeutic interventions defied categorization, but 'Ericksonian hypnosis' is the name commonly given to the particular style of hypnotherapy he used and taught. Erickson was more of a discoverer than an inventor.

Dr Erickson treated symptoms as signals. What is it saying? What is it telling you? You want to recognise these signals, listen to them and utilise them.

"If your opponent tries to pull you, let him pull. Don't pull against him; pull in unison with him". – O Sensei

You could say that as he pulled the cow's tail that then caused it to go in the opposite direction and forward into the barn, it wasn't blending or going with the flow. However he was blending with the cow's pattern of going in the opposite direction to where it is pulled.

Although initially Bandler and Grinder modelled three therapists they went on to model excellence in other areas and showed that the same principles are used. They presupposed that people were not born with a god-given talent but had acquired their skills through learning and experience and therefore others can learn to do the same things as well. Their job was to discover what precisely the skills were, how to learn and use them and be able to teach them to others.

Contemporary books, "Outliers", by Malcolm Gladwell, "Bounce" by Matthew Syid and "The Talent Code", by Daniel Coyle confirm the idea that skills can be modelled and learnt and are not dependant on "talent", something that the authors claim does not exist, and that they have discovered this via modelling those people who are the best in their fields.

Bandler and Grinder did their studies of excellent people by what is known in NLP as 2nd position modelling, standing in the other person's shoes, micro mirroring them so they were able to pick up "intuitions" about what these excellent performers were feeling and experiencing while performing their particular skill and as a result of this absorption process they were able to repeat what the exemplar was doing. They may not have had conscious coding of how to do it but they could do it.

American Political Scientist Herbert Simon says the following about intuition:

"Valid intuitions develop when experts have learned to recognise familiar elements in a new situation and to act in a manner that is appropriate to it."

I once trained with Michael Field, an Aikido Sensei in Melbourne, Australia who when he discovered I was a NLP Coach told me he had done some NLP training himself because he wanted to get conscious coding of what he was doing successfully with his students, find out what the steps were and add that to his teaching for his Aikido students as well as others.

More conscious understanding comes from explicit modelling which involves observing and listening to the exemplars, dissecting their language patterns, questioning them about their behaviours, how they process information, what they are paying attention to, what their beliefs are and what their internal state is, i.e. how they feel while doing this particular skill and by standing in their shoes, getting inside the exemplar's skin and mind while they were performing these activities and literally taking them on. Andy Hathaway Sensei thinks of himself as stepping into or being a "ghost" and wrapping himself around Saito Sensei while he is doing techniques.

A lot of their patterns will be revealed in their language. For instance one person may talk about dealing with a problem and another's emphasis may be on their goal. These are different motivation strategies of moving away from some sort of problem or difficulty and moving towards a goal, one of Charles Faulkner's six key-steps in achievement, and if I were modelling them, in order to perform their skill, initially I would need to match them and use whichever strategy they are using. Once I can do what they are able to do I can experiment with honing and streamlining the strategy.

Many years ago I modelled 3 people who said that they had given up smoking easily. I did 3 interviews or modelling sessions with each person and when I asked them how they had stopped smoking easily all three of them initially said they didn't do anything, they just stopped.

So I took them back to that moment and contextualised it by asking them where they were and what they were doing. Slowly they were able to give me a lot of information that they hadn't consciously been aware of and didn't consider to be important, like setting a goal and having a deadline or as I like to think about it, a lifeline.

Incidentally there is a "health warning" with modelling. The more we match someone, the more we can take on their feelings and this can include symptoms of any illness or disability. NLP has strategies to build "life lines", a rock climbing metaphor, that is present during the modelling process. This usually means setting up some arrangement with your unconscious mind to ensure you can come back to yourself without taking on any symptoms.

Milton Erickson had Polio when he was younger and was in a lot of pain throughout his life. Bandler and Grinder took time to build themselves "life lines" before they went to work with Erickson to ensure they didn't take on any of his symptoms or physical traits.

They could certainly sound like Erickson who had a distinctive way of speaking. Perhaps this is how mimics are able to imitate others so well because they are modelling them and become them. That would be an interesting project, to model mimics and maybe its already been done. I suspect there is another piece to that, happening unconsciously. So for modelling to be an ecological process so that we can fully immerse ourselves in the exemplars we are modelling, we need to know we are safe and our lifelines will take care of us and bring us back cleanly to ourselves in the present.

When we are training on the mat we are not only matching the other persons movements, we are also getting inside their skin and getting information as to their intention.

The modelling of the three therapists revealed the language patterns they were using when working with their clients. People delete, distort and generalise in their use of language so Bandler and Grinder developed a NLP model of language called the "Meta Model" in order to retrieve, clarify and specify the deleted, distorted and generalised information.

For example I have used a deletion in my sentence with the word "People". Using the Meta Model we might want to get this specified by asking: "Which people specifically?"

This work on language was published in 1975, was the first NLP book and is entitled "The Structure of Magic".

The process of modelling is the heart of NLP. Stepping in and getting a sense of what the other person is doing and copying or mirroring them. This implicit modelling is done from a "not knowing" state. There isn't any questioning, just doing. This is also how Aikido is taught and learnt. There is some explanation and demonstration and then it involves physical action. You have to do it, experiential learning, and it is learnt when, after enough repetitions and corrections, and the "students" have got it, as dancers say, "in the muscle".

"I never paid as much attention to what Sensei said as to what he did. You could ask him all the questions you wanted and never understand his answers. He would just show you and say something to the effect of "It's done like this." – Koichi Tohei Sensei

Obviously this process of learning can be sped up and refined by utilising the principles of excellence, particularly the idea that effective learning is state dependant and also by having an awareness of the different stages and levels of learning. Some people learn or attempt to learn in ways that are not useful by doing the same thing (s) over and over and beating themselves up when feedback or coaching is offered, so they are constantly in a less than useful state for learning.

They don't understand that mistakes are the places where they learn most when they take on board and utilise the feedback. When they change the way they think about feedback and reframe it as learning opportunities, then they will be in a more useful state and accelerate their learning.

The information that is obtained from the modelling is streamlined and tested so that only what is essential for the skill to work is taught to others. They went on to model excellence in other fields such as business, education, art, sport and health.

"We are what we repeatedly do. Excellence, then, is not an act but a habit." – Aristotle

Psychologist Peter Gray has kindly given permission to quote from an article he has written for "Psychology Today" based on research done by Anthropologists on learning in Hunter-Gatherer cultures

The children learn without being taught.

Although hunter-gatherer children must learn an enormous amount, hunter-gatherers have nothing like school. Adults do not establish a curriculum, or attempt to motivate children to learn, or give lessons, or monitor children's progress. When asked how children learn what they need to know, hunter-gatherer adults invariably answer with words that mean essentially: "They teach themselves through their observations, play, and exploration." Occasionally an adult might offer a word of advice or demonstrate how to do something better, such as how to shape an arrowhead, but such help is given only when the child clearly desires it. Adults do not initiate, direct, or interfere with children's activities. Adults do not show any evidence of worry about their children's education; millennia of experience have proven to them that children are experts at educating themselves.

The children are afforded enormous amounts of time to play and explore.

The freedom that hunter-gatherer children enjoy to pursue their own interests comes partly from the adults' understanding that such pursuits are the surest path to education.

In response to our question about how much time children had for play, the anthropologists we surveyed were unanimous in indicating that the hunter-gatherer children they observed were free to play most if not all of the day, every day. Typical responses are the following:

- "Batek children were free to play nearly all the time; no one expected children to do serious work until they were in their late teens." (Karen Endicott.)

- "Both girls and boys [among the Nharo] had almost all day every day free to play." (Alan Barnard.)

- "Efé boys were free to play nearly all the time until age 15-17; for girls most of the day, in between a few errands and some babysitting, was spent in play." (Robert Bailey.)

- "! Kung children played from dawn to dusk." (Nancy Howell.)

Children observe adults' activities and incorporate them into their play. They are modelling the adults and are learning by mirroring and doing.

The Hunter-Gatherer children are "stealing" information from the adults by watching and doing and only need to ask when they need help. What strategies do you have for learning and learning how to learn?

One of the things we need to learn in Aikido is to eradicate redundant body language so we have to firstly become aware of those mostly unconscious movements, mindfulness of the body if you will, and then unlearn a lot of the movements that are wired into our systems at an unconscious level and we have to, as Jung said; *"make the unconscious, conscious"*. This is the purpose of training, to get the mental awareness via feedback from the instructor, Sensei or training partner, hone what we are doing and take on new ways.

We can think about what we want instead of redundant body movement, visualising ourselves being still, ready and relaxed and then we can, as well as fixing ourselves, move toward being relaxed and ready to move. With enough training this then becomes automatic. It is the "programming" part of Neuro Linguistic Programming, wiring in new patterns.

The following is an example of unlearning and wiring in or as athletes say, grooving in, a new way until it is habitulised and we no longer have to think about how we do it.

Cross your arms as you normally do, e.g. in my case left arm over right arm.

Now change it to right arm over left arm. Not so smooth an operation, is it? Keep practising and usually after 5 or 6 times it starts to become automatic, you no longer have to think about it so much.

This is what we are doing throughout our lives, running learnt and wired-in patterns, some of which are not useful. The good news is that when you become aware of them, you can begin to change them.

Generally we have been taught to do exercise and sports, building fitness and muscle strength. When you are confronted by a strong grip you tend to do things like raise your shoulders and gather your strength to overcome the grip. You sort of take a run at it instead of moving from your centre and in that moment you are giving an opening to the opponent who can match your upward movement by pushing up, blocking you and taking your balance.

We learn new patterns instead and you can do this by remembering times when you had that sense of stillness and a time you were relaxed and practice bringing these states to the present. What are you like when you are still and relaxed? Visualise yourself doing that and then associate into it. This is what we are doing in coaching, freeing up those moments of tension, where you are stuck, so that you can step back into flow.

"Be like water making its way through cracks. Do not be assertive, but adjust to the object, and you shall find a way around or through it. If nothing within you stays rigid, outward things will disclose themselves.

Now, water can flow or it can crash. Be water, my friend." – Bruce Lee

John Grinder said that the 3 curses of western civilisation are:

- Muscle tension
- Foveal (tunnel) vision
- Too much internal dialogue

Bandler and Grinder discovered that excellent performers in different fields had things in common in what they did when working with their clients or performing and that there are three essential ingredients that need to be present in order to be successful in any context.

- Outcome – to know what you want, your direction, your goal.
- Awareness – to notice the responses you are getting and whether you are on the right track.
- Flexibility – the ability to adjust your behaviour appropriately.

There may be other things present but it is essential for these three components to always be there and Bandler and Grinder called this:

"A Success Strategy"

The ingredients can be used to create a successful meal whatever else there is in the mix. NLP is not about content; it is about process, how we do something and **outcome**, **awareness** and **flexibility** are the essential ingredients.

Of course there are many components inside these three ingredients so lets have a more detailed look at the components of this success strategy.

KNOW WHAT YOU WANT

Harmonisation is the goal of Aikido.

Aikido 10th Dan, Koichi Tohei famously remarked that the most important lesson he learned from founder O Sensei, Morihei Ueshiba, was how to relax.

If you read books about and by Samurai they have a clear outcome (goal) that has nothing to do with swords and fighting. What so many of history's greatest warriors stress as key to success and optimal performance is:

"Being calm."

And it wasn't one random samurai mentioning it off the cuff.

We're talking about some of the greatest samurai who ever lived writing about it over and over for five hundred years:

Samurai trained relentlessly. They strongly believed you should always "be prepared" (they were like the deadliest Boy Scouts imaginable).

Research shows preparation reduces fear because when things get tense, you don't have to think.

I was working in a College in London using NLP to teach learning strategies and one afternoon I was scheduled to work with a group to deliver some Presentation Skills. I walked into the room and reminded them what was planned for this particular session, i.e. strategies for Presentation Skills and one young lady immediately stood up in front of me and said:

"Oh no, I have got this terrible nervousness. Can you help me?"

I could certainly hear some of that nervousness in her voice. She stared at me intensely, waiting for my reply.

"You have some nervousness" I replied. "What's causing you to feel nervous?"

"We have to go for interviews at Universities and there is usually a panel of people and I have this terrible nervousness", she repeated and continued to stare at me.

I paused and thought about what she had said and then asked her:

"Do you know what nervousness is?"

"Yes" she replied and then began to describe this nervousness. She placed her hand on her abdomen and said:

"It is a feeling just here and it goes up into my chest. It's horrible and I don't think I can go."

By this time some of her colleagues had stepped up beside her and listened as I said:

"Maybe that feeling that you call nervousness is your unconscious mind letting you know it's time to prepare."

I watched her and saw her pupils dilate as she processed this statement. This can indicate that someone is going into an altered state as in hypnosis and it's also in our everyday language when we talk about "being wide eyed". I waited and eventually she focussed on me again and she said:

"Great, can you show us how to do it then?"

So I went on to go through the presentation skills with them.

Before this conversation the young lady couldn't think about doing the interview or the class on presentation skills because the feeling she called nervousness was overwhelming her and stopping her from doing anything.

What I had done was to reframe the word and meaning of the word, nervousness, as a communication or signal to let her know it was time to prepare. This is also known as "proper naming" where we come up with another word that has a similar meaning but is a bit more positive. Once she understood and accepted that, then she could and wanted to take action to prepare and learn how to do an interview well.

We completed the session successfully and she never once referred to her "nervousness" again. This is the nature of change. It can happen in a moment and then it's often as if the client can't remember the problem they had. The brain can't go backwards.

"Prepare for what's difficult when it's easy." – Lao Szu

It's important to realise that we don't respond to someone's "problem" by saying something like:

"Well pull yourself together, you can do this". This statement is well intended but is coming from someone else's map and is a mismatch to that person's experience. They have a strong feeling that is stopping them and it is essential to acknowledge that and then attempt to lead them in some way.

The Process of "Reframing"

"When you change the way you look at things, the things you look at change" – Wayne Dyer

We literally put a different frame around the issue thereby transforming its meaning. NLP says that all behaviour is useful in some context. Those feelings we call emotions become signals, communications and messages.

- What is the purpose of the problem?
- What else could the problem mean?
- Where and/or how would this behaviour be useful?
- What is the positive intention of the problem?

By addressing these questions you can change your perception and consequently any negative internal state and this can then allow you to move forward.

The most important "Principle of Excellence" – State (how you feel) – The young woman was in a state that stopped her from doing anything.

In any context we always start with a goal and ask ourselves" What do I want? What is my outcome here? Knowing what you want is certainly one of the most important principles and our state, i.e. how we feel is equally very important.

HOW WE FEEL WILL DETERMINE HOW WELL WE PERFORM

Contemporary thinking and research backs this up and shows how we feel will determine how well we perform. We will have a look at and get a sense of how we can choose what we want to feel, later in the book.

Bearing in mind the idea of high performance states, it's useful to have a way of getting into those states before you embark on something, be it dealing with a problem, a performance or a piece of work with someone else such as coaching. The following is one way and is called:

Finding Your Zone

We go in and out of different "states" throughout the day depending on what we are doing, what is happening to us and what we are thinking. Any one of these can and does change how we feel. State or internal state is another way of talking about how we feel.

When you're watching TV, or reading a book, or driving a car, your thoughts drift away, almost as if your conscious mind was taking a break as in Hypnosis.

Have you ever had the experience of driving somewhere and when you arrived you realised you had no conscious memory of doing the journey. So who was driving?

It is well known that how we feel will have an important effect on how well, or otherwise, we perform in our lives, whether it is communicating with friends, family or colleagues or engaging in some other sort of activity.

Sports people are well aware of this and a lot of their training is about managing and improving their "mental state" so as to be able to perform at a high level. This is referred to as "Being in the Zone" where time seems to slow down and actions are performed with ease.

Scientific research has shown that how we think can have a dramatic effect on our health. The beliefs we hold about ourselves are linked to the immune system and can affect our ability to deal with illness. Beliefs are our filters on the world and they are self fulfilling so are powerful ways to get what we want with our health, as in the placebo effect, and materially.

"Nothing is more wondrous about the fifteen billion neurons in the human brain than their ability to convert thoughts, hopes, ideas, and attitudes into chemical substances. Everything begins, therefore, with belief: What we believe is the most important option of all." – Norman Cousins.

Thinking about positive or negative things such as memories, traumas and past "failure" will cause chemical changes in the brain and therefore also the body. The same is true when you visualise yourselves achieving, recall pleasant memories and focus on your successes. This sort of thinking will cause production of "feel good" chemicals like endorphins and serotonin.

Research has shown that the brain chemicals that are produced by people in a powerful position, that sense of power that they get, are the same as produced from sex and drugs, hence the reluctance of some of these people to give up their position of power. They are literally addicted to their chemical structure of the feeling of power and perhaps the reluctance to give it up leads to the idea that power sometimes corrupts.

There are many ways for people to learn how they can get into positive, useful and high performance states. The following is one way, only takes a few minutes and when done as a daily practice will enable you to access a focussed and relaxed state, which will help to bring you back to your centre, be grounded and live your life in a relaxed and focussed way.

- Sit or stand in a comfortable position with both feet flat on the floor and your spine erect but relaxed. Check that your breathing is regular and from the belly. (Shallow, short or rapid breathing from the chest could indicate that you are in a stressed mode.)

- Bring your attention to the soles of your feet (i.e. put your "mind" into your feet). Become aware of the universe of sensations in the bottoms of your feet...and feel the surface of your heels, toes, arches and the balls of your feet.

- Begin to expand your awareness now... to include the physical reality (the 3-dimensional space) of your feet and then move up through your lower legs, knees, thighs, pelvis and hips. Become aware of your belly centre and say to your self "I am here".

- Continuing to stay aware of your lower body...and move your awareness up through your solar plexus, spine, lungs, rib cage and chest. Focus on your heart centre and say to your self, "I am open".

- Expand your attention to move up through your shoulders, upper arms, elbows, lower arms, wrists, hands and fingers, and up through your neck, throat, face, skull and brain. Bring your awareness to the centre in your head, behind your eyes, and say to yourself, "I am awake, I am alert and clear".

- Staying in contact with the on-going physical sensations in your body and the three centres become aware of all the space above you, reaching into the sky: all of the space below you, going into the centre of the earth. All of the space to your left, all of the space to your right all of the space behind you and all of the space in front of you. Say to your self "I am ready".

Back to the success strategy from page 80.

WELL FORMING AN OUTCOME

"Obstacles are the things you notice when you take your eyes off your goals." – Henry Ford

SMART, Specified, Measurable, Acceptable, Realistic and Time Bound is okay for specific targets but going for direction is a much better strategy.

The brain is a goal seeking or psycho-cybernetic organism, see Maxwell Maltz's book of the same name on which some motivational and self-help experts have based their work. Give the brain a goal and it will go after it. This gave birth to the idea of visualisation.

NLP goals allow for much more freedom and this is understandable as a core value of NLP is freedom. Connecting the goal with your senses is necessary because it enables you to have a powerful feeling attached and this is also an ingredient of motivation. Second, it checks with the ecology of the goal that will have an impact on the rest of your life.

According to Robert B Cialdini in his book, "Influence: The Psychology of Persuasion", it is important to write down goals and more than that to make it public particularly if it is about some sort of personal change such as stopping smoking.

Whenever someone takes a stand that is visible to others there is a motivation or commitment to maintain that stand in order to look like a consistent person. The more public a stand, the more reluctant you will be to change it.

It is essential that an outcome is "well formed", is achievable, and has an evidence procedure that lets you know you are on track to achieving your outcome and the following steps will enable you to do this:

1. **Positive:** Make sure the outcome is framed and stated in the positive. Quite often when I ask someone what he or she wants they will tell me what they don't want. This is OK because it is information and that can be useful to know, and it is important to then know what you want instead, stated in the positive and by doing this you are beginning to build pictures of that goal in your mind. This change in the way you think can and will, in itself, facilitate benefits for you.

   If you are working with someone and when you ask him or her what he or she wants, they tell you what they don't want, e.g.

   "I don't want to feel bad every time a bill comes through the letterbox."

   Acknowledge that by repeating that statement back to them,

   "So you don't want to feel bad every time a bill arrives and what do you want instead of that?"

   If you don't get a positive outcome from this repeat the process until you do and then you have an outcome that is stated in the positive.

2. **Achievement:** What is the evidence that lets you know you are achieving or have achieved your outcome?

   - What will you see, hear and feel to let you know you have achieved your outcome?

- What would others see, hear and feel that lets them know you have achieved your outcome?

3. **Context:** When do you want this and with whom? When don't you want it?

4. **Ecology:** When you achieve this goal would there be anything you are losing? Does this goal fit in with who you are and who you are becoming?

5. **Resources:** Do you have the resources to initiate getting and maintaining this outcome? A well-formed outcome cannot be dependant on what someone else does because they may not do it.

AWARENESS

A young man went to learn the art of the sword from a master swordsman. He expected to be taught techniques but was asked to cook, sweep up and generally keep the place clean.

Whilst doing this he would often be surprised by the Sensei who would suddenly appear and strike him with a stick.

After several months of doing nothing but chores and getting surprised and struck with the stick, the student complained that he had come to train and learn the secrets and techniques of the sword.

The sensei told him he had already been learning by becoming more aware until he was able to avoid most of the sensei's strikes and now that he had learnt awareness he could begin to learn the sword.

One of the important learnings in Aikido is to be aware of what is going on around you, all the time. Even at the end of a technique there is a moments pause of 1 or 2 seconds where the finishing position is held. This is one of the 4 main principles of Aikido and is called "Zanshin" meaning something like "Remaining Spirit". We learn to be martial, aware and ready at all times without tension and paranoia.

It is interesting to observe people and indeed our-selves when we are performing an activity like sports or a presentation and notice our automatic responses when things don't go well.

For instance watch a football game, a tennis match or your mates playing golf and see what they do when they miss a goal, fail to get a return over the net or miss an easy golf putt.

We instantly put our hands over our heads and/or stifle a shriek with a hand. Our heads go down and lowering the head can be a sign of loss, defeat, shame, etc. Hence the expressions such as 'don't let your head drop', and 'don't let your head go down' or "Keep your head up". You can see this especially in sports and competitive activities. Head down also tends to cause your shoulders and upper back to slump, increasing the signs of weakness at that moment.

When hands are clasping the head, it is like a protective helmet against some disaster, problem or calamity and frequent examples of this can be clearly seen when footballers miss a shot on goal or a tennis player nets a return and the more important that moment is in the match or performance, the more extreme the reaction.

You will also see from the diagram in the Appendices on page 280/81, illustrating eye movements, that the position down and to the right with the eyes and the body puts us in the kinaesthetic zone, i.e. we are accessing our feelings and in the case of "failure" these are negative feelings and not conducive to excellent performance unless, and this is the key bit, you are aware that innovative learning comes out of failure and mistakes.

As Matthew Sayid says in his book "Black Box Thinking": *"Evolution is driven by failure"*.

The mistakes are an opportunity to learn and improve your performance and be successful.

I was recently watching Manchester City playing Real Madrid in the semi final of the Champions league where they lost 1 – 0. These are two of the best football (soccer) teams in Europe, fielding world class players and I lost count of the number of times I saw players making these gestures of disappointment and reinforcing their negative feelings.

We sort of take ourselves outside of the interaction we are engaged in, be it football, tennis, aikido or a communication in a relationship or negotiation. There have been times when I have seen players quickly take a throw-in or free kick while opposing players are still engaged in these gestures, and sometimes scoring because of the opening given.

The opposing players "were not ready". Having an understanding of our unconscious movements means we can begin to install other strategies in our thinking to deal with those moments such as the meaning we make, i.e.

- Is it a failure or an opportunity to learn?
- Be more careful with what we say to ourselves.
- Appreciate how close we got to success.
- The most important learning is embedded in the "failure"

Training in Aikido is "as if" you are in combat so when things go wrong, making these sorts of body movements and gestures and "not being ready" is not an option because you will have given an opening and that would mean defeat.

In combat or training on the mat you have to be present all the time and when things are not working stay present and connected so that you can blend with the situation and your demonstration of being present will keep you ready and in the case of a "real" situation, it may be enough to stop anything further happening.

Building this awareness and being mindful takes a lot of training until it becomes "wired in" and is a natural thing to do. I think this is an area that is not generally addressed and in terms of excellence is the difference that can make the difference in succeeding or not, whether it's in sports or business.

What would it be like if you worked or played "as if" your life depended on it? How sharp would you be then?

What strategies can you use in the moment when you have not achieved your outcome?

It could be useful for you to examine your strategy for dealing with a situation when it hasn't worked out.

What happens in your thinking?

- Do you see internal pictures of past failures or see the consequences of not achieving?
- Are you hearing anything like negative feedback from yourself or others? What's the tone of voice like?

These are internal strategies and will produce an unresourceful feeling that is demonstrated in your body language.

Zanshin is an Aikido term and means remaining mind and is practised as general awareness or mindfulness of one's surroundings of which uke (your training partner) is just a small part.

The dojo is an ideal place to practice and develop spatial awareness, as can be, working with horses, playing football, wild animals, war zones, crossing the street, driving a car, being employed as a professional protector of any kind, the list is endless.

For the true Aikidoka the decision to address Zanshin – spatial awareness with the importance it deserves is a requirement, not a mystical ambiguity to be mostly ignored. Zanshin is maintaining your connection to others and your surroundings at all times.

The mat in a Dojo (training space) is at the neurological level of environment, a sacred space; metaphorically it is like the battlefield, and is a place where people come to train in a potentially dangerous martial art in a safe way. In order to do this we must respect and be able to trust our training partner and learn the art of providing a specific attack, receiving the technique that is appropriate for that attack and taking ukemi (break falls) so as to facilitate each other's learning. So even in a combat situation, albeit training, there is cooperation.

One of the greatest dangers is if someone "switches off" and this is when an accident can happen because people are taking falls and sometimes using weapons and a lack of awareness can mean a collision and possible injury.

Safety is a priority and students soon develop the awareness that keeps you safe both on and off the mat. In more than 30 years of Aikido practice I have only seen a few minor "accidents" and this is a testament to the Dojos I have trained in and the aikidoka that I have trained with.

In NLP we learn the importance of putting our attention on the outside and noticing peoples' non-verbal signals (body language) as well as taking in information from the environment we are in and later you will learn how this can keep you safe and is as important as any martial art technique.

The environment in NLP Training and coaching also requires the building of a safe space and in a one to one situation the coach's outcome is to create one relationship, rather than two separate people, in a communication loop.

Equally important is self-awareness and mindfulness, noticing what is happening on the inside and being able to make adjustments in your own thinking. Timothy Galway talks about this in his book "The Inner Game".

He was a Tennis player and he noticed that after he started meditating his tennis got better without any extra training to improve his technique. He went on to write a series of "Inner Game" books applying his ideas to both the inner and outer game in a variety of contexts such as sports and business.

"In every human endeavour there are two arenas of engagement: the outer and the inner. The outer game is played on an external arena to overcome external obstacles to reach an external goal. The inner game takes place within the mind of the player and is played against such obstacles as fear, self-doubt, lapses in focus, and limiting concepts or assumptions. The inner game is played to overcome the self-imposed obstacles that prevent an individual or team from accessing their full potential." – Timothy Galway

Milton Erickson would say:

"Never underestimate the power of the mind. First things happen on the inside then they happen on the outside."

The process that Musashi studied and lived by during his life was Zen, which teaches that life, must be seized in the moment not before or after.

"The meaning of life is in the daily living of It." – Tolstoy

Eckhart Tolle is a spiritual teacher, spiritual guide and author. He writes about being in the present in his book "The Power of Now."

Tolle writes that:

"The most significant thing that can happen to a human being is the separation process of thinking and awareness" and that awareness is *"the space in which thoughts exist"* Tolle says that *"the primary cause of unhappiness is never the situation but your thoughts about it"*.

Similar to what William Shakespeare's Hamlet said:

"There is nothing either good or bad, but thinking makes it so."

FLEXIBILITY

Having an evidence procedure means you can be aware of whether you are on track to achieving your outcome and if not, having that awareness enables you to change what you are doing in some way to get you back on track.

"If you always do the same thing you will always get the same result. If what you are doing is not working then you need to do something different."

An airliner doesn't fly in a straight line. It is constantly being moved off course by the wind and its direction is continuously adjusted to bring it back on track. If it does not respond to feedback it will, like us, eventually be travelling way off course.

A strong oak tree will break or be uprooted given a strong enough wind but a Willow tree has both strength and flexibility and will bend to the ground and then come back to its center as the wind subsides.

LEARNING

Pablo Casals, the famous Spanish cellist lived to be 97 years of age and when he reached 95, a young reporter threw him a question:

"Mr Casals, you are 95 and the greatest cellist that ever lived. Why do you still practice six hours a day?"

And Mr Casals answered,

"Because I think I'm making progress."

Miyamoto Musashi said that a 1000 days practice was discipline and 10,000 days refinement. In order to learn anything we have to do it over and over, gradually getting better at it until we no longer have to think about what we are doing. We can just do it automatically. It is said that the path to mastery in any field requires 10,000 hours practice, usually equivalent to a decade.

Matthew Sayid shows in his book: "Bounce" that most experts, champions in all fields started when they were very young and had done their 10,000 hours by their early teens. He says that mastery is about practice not "talent" and more than that, opportunity to practice, and in a special way that he calls "deep practice". Mistakes are worked on until they are corrected and effort rather than intelligence is praised.

In Sanskrit the word for practice is Abhyasa. It translates to, *'persistent, consistent effort, practiced over a long period of time'*. It does not mean practice when we find time for it. It does not mean wait until you attend your next class. It is a fiercely focused commitment necessary to create a change.

There are 4 stages of learning:

1. Unconscious incompetence – we don't know that we don't know until we try to do the behaviour.

   Think about trying to ride a bike for the first time. You may have seen others riding bikes and think it is easy to do. However as soon as you get on the bike you immediately discover how difficult it is and probably lose your balance.

2. Conscious incompetence – we have begun to learn to do it and have discovered that we don't yet know how.

   There are so many things to do. You have to steer, push the pedals round, and use the brakes and gears, look to the front and sides and as well as all that learn to keep your balance. This information overload is what makes it feel so difficult.

3. Conscious competence – after a bit of practice we are beginning to get the hang of it.

   As long as you keep on practising you will improve, bit by bit

4. Unconscious competence – this is the magic place where our continuous practice means that we reach the point where we have got it in the muscles and do not have to think about what we are doing and it has become automatic.

Stage 2 is the area that most of us find difficult because it is all new and requires us to deal with and put together a lot of new pieces of information consciously until we begin to reach a certain level of competency. Stage 2 can feel uncomfortable as you are juggling lots of new information and it is the place and time where people talk about "confusion" because of this sense of overload, but it is also the stage where you can do the most learning when you persevere.

Confusion is not a state of not knowing but rather new information that you have not yet organised.

"The illiterate of the 21st century will not be those who cannot read and write, but those who cannot learn, unlearn and relearn."
– Alvin Toffler

Small steps are more useful when learning new stuff and this helps us expand our comfort zones. Sometimes when we are out of our comfort zone we retreat because it's unfamiliar and we don't know what to do.

"Failure" is a learning point and learning continues when we keep going. People fail because they stop trying. They get discouraged and stop so be happy about stepping outside your comfort zone because it's an important learning point.

In his book "The Talent Code" Daniel Coyle says:

"Nothing you can do - talking, thinking, reading, imagining – is more effective in building skill than executing the action, firing the impulse down the nerve fiber, fixing errors, honing the circuit".

The 4 stages of learning is not a fixed model because we are always adding to and refining our skills. When we have learnt something well enough for it to be automatic and then add or change something in what we are doing in order to improve, we go back to stage 2 in the learning process and have to repeat the behaviour over and over, incorporating the new point and thinking about what we are doing consciously until we move to stage 3 and then stage 4 where the skill once again becomes automatic and you are unconsciously competent again.

Learning and mastery are on-going processes. There is no fixed point where we can say: "I have got it now" and that's it, we stop learning. It is only by remaining on the path that we discover there is so much more, like the layers of the onion.

According to one of his students, Ulf Evanas Aikido Shihan once said:

"I have been practising Aikido since 40 years and I can find some new thing during every training."

A Shodan, first black belt in Aikido means you have completed an apprenticeship and are now a beginner, not an expert or Master.

I often experience this "step back" in the learning process in my Aikido training. We learn techniques so well we don't have to think about what we are doing and then the Sensei offers some small point and the automatic programme is interrupted taking us back to conscious incompetence, stage 2 in the learning stages where once again we are feeling uncomfortable and awkward and having to consciously think about what we are doing.

"When any real progress is made, we unlearn and learn anew what we thought we knew before." – Henry David Thoreau

Josh Waitzkin calls this "investment in loss." If we are not willing to let go of how we usually operate then we will never move forward.

I think this may be one of the reasons why people give up on learning anything. They reach a certain standard and then find themselves back at stage 2 every time they incorporate new information and learnings and feel uncomfortable and give up, thinking that they can't learn that particular skill or they don't want to put in the practice and sometimes get annoyed because they can't perform at their usual level and feel they are going backwards. One thing I have learned is that when I encounter those feelings it means I am learning.

We have to repeat the technique incorporating the new piece enough times in order for you to get back to stage 3, conscious competence and then stage 4, unconscious competence. As a teacher it is important to know about and understand this principle so that you can be aware of and help people manage their learning states.

"Iron is full of impurities that weaken it; through forging, it becomes steel and is transformed into a razor-sharp sword. Human beings develop in the same fashion."

– O Sensei, Morihei Ueshiba

O Sensei taught for many years and over the years acquired many students, some of whom eventually produced their own books on Aikido. O Sensei didn't codify the techniques in detail when he was teaching and it was up to his students to deconstruct them, break down the techniques into smaller chunks and codify the movements. This was mainly done by his long-term student, Saito Sensei and is the job of the modeller and the test is always in the teaching. Can you do it yourself and teach it to others?

Can you learn it, understand the difference that makes the difference, be able to do it yourself and then teach it to others?

NLP modelling unpacks the underlying structure of human behaviour and how we think so that we can learn ways that will be useful and even more effective in achieving your outcomes.

Now if you can imagine yourself as the ideal learner, a person that can look at any situation and extract the key piece of learning that will improve your performance, what would that look and feel like? What questions would you ask of yourself to get the best from you and how would it feel if you were doing that?

THINKING AND INFLUENCE

Change how you think and it will change how you feel and that changes what you can do. How do we think? We take in information from the world around us through our senses. There is no other way to get information and therefore, regardless of the content, thinking has a structure

We think in pictures, sounds, feelings, smells and tastes.

Each of these senses, as we process them, has qualities. For instance our internal pictures have a size, big or small, distance, near or far, location, in front, to the sides, up or down as well as colour or B/W, sharpness and framed or panorama. They can also be dissociated where we see ourselves in the picture or associated which is as if we are in the picture.

Our internal voices have volume, speed, tone and tempo as well as location.

Feelings have qualities such as touch, location, temperature and the qualities of rough, smooth, wet, dry; internal feelings we call emotions, that are about something, like happy, sad, angry, calm etc. and balance. Feelings do not stay still. They have movement.

A lot of these qualities can be heard in our language, for example we talk about:

Having bright futures, looking forward, looking up to someone, putting things behind us, getting a distance on something or finding a different perspective, putting a gloss on things, seeing things through rose tinted glasses, things getting on top of us, feeling overwhelmed, often caused by having too many internal pictures at the same time.

You can probably think of some more phrases we use and all of them describe our mostly unconscious internal world.

There is an acronym for the sensory system – **VAKOG** – visual, auditory, kinaesthetic, olfactory and gustatory. In NLP these are known as representational channels or modalities and make up the representational or sensory system.

The interesting thing is that even though the only way we can all get information is through our senses, we tend to do it in different ways to create our own inner map of the world. For instance some people will use the visual system more while others will prefer the kinaesethic and/or auditory system and this will show up in the words people use as well as in their physiology.

Marshall McLuhan, a Canadian philosopher of communication theory believed that different cultures preferred the use of different representational channels and that cultures are deeply influenced by the representational channel that is preferred by that culture. Conflicts between groups can come from cultural differences and values.

NLP Trainer Robert Dilts has run courses where he takes groups to places like The British Museum and observes and discusses how Art from different cultures demonstrates the representational channel that is preferred by that culture.

We all use these sensory channels or modalities and we tend to do it differently because we have developed our skills more in one channel and will therefore have a preference in that channel and it is where we will default particularly when under pressure.

This has profound implications for learning, memory, creativity and how we perceive and deal with both the inner and outer world. In western cultures the least used part of the sensory system is the auditory channel, which may explain the birth of MTV, as the music on its own, was not enough.

"We learn by example and by direct experience because there are real limits to the adequacy of verbal instruction." – Malcolm Gladwell

Obviously in a learning environment, as a teacher, we are working with people who may have a range of sensory system preferences and the best way to deal with that is to present the information in all systems.

When John Grinder was once asked if he had any regrets about any of the NLP material that he and Richard Bandler had presented during their initial workshops and books he replied that he thought that how some people had taken the VAKOG model and labelled others or themselves as visual, auditory or kinaesthetic, which are identity level descriptions, was very limiting.

This is a confusion of neuro logical levels. A person is not "visual" which is a statement about their identity but has a preference to process information through the visual channel more than the other channels. Something they do rather than who they are so it is not fixed.

Nobody uses only the visual channel or the auditory or kinaesthetic channels. We all use all channels but will have preferences and we are more developed in one or two of the representational channels. You can develop your abilities in the channels you use least by way of practise and improve your abilities that would mean you are then operating out of a richer map.

When people are learning some sort of physical activity like Aikido they cannot use only the kinaesthetic system to learn. It is certainly useful to be in touch (kinaesthetic description) with your own body and you also need to watch demonstrations, be able to visualise and listen to instructions and explanations as well as doing the activity so the term "kinaesthetic learner" is incorrect on two levels; confusion of neuro logical levels as previously mentioned, and the fact that you will use the other channels to take in information visually and auditorily.

A "kinaesthetic learner" may have difficulty translating verbal descriptions from visual words like see, clear, bright etc to kinaesthetic words like sense, hold, move and feel.

The VAKOG words we use in language are known as predicates and you can **see and digest** a list of them in Appendices on page 279/80.

When these students with kinaesthetic preferences hear words in other than their preferred system they have to go inside and "translate" them into their preferred system and while they are doing this they are missing what's going on so they always have gaps in their learning and are thus sometimes labelled "slow learners". It would be worthwhile to be able to help others to identify the representational channel that they use most. You can then go onto developing your skills in your less used channels.

"The single most influential variable is the relationship between the student and the teacher. If the relationship is strong and constitutes a stable context for the student to learn, that student will learn."

John Grinder wrote this in the foreword to his brother Michael's excellent book: "Righting the Educational Conveyor Belt".

Michael Grinder says that in a typical classroom of 30 students 22 will have abilities in VAK, 4 – 6 are translators and these students are using mostly Visual only, Auditory only and Kinesthetic only. "Mostly K only" makes up the largest of the 26% dropout rate amongst students and 2 – 3 will have other interfering factors such as social or learning difficulties.

When someone is teaching or leading a group they can present information in all channels in their language, show what they mean in some way like symbols, notes or as in my case, Mindmaps and demonstrate or devise ways for students to physically participate. That means they can match everyone's learning style and keep delivery of new information to 10 minutes or less and then recycle.

When learning we can also use the principles of modelling to study and get inside an excellent performer. The use of these modelling skills is at the heart of accelerated learning and this is an example of where mostly kinaesthetic learning can take place. You can match or mirror the other person's movements until you find you can do it.

According to Gregory Bateson there are 3 levels of learning:

- Learning
- Learning how to learn
- Learning about learning how to learn

The following is an article published in Aikido Journal in 1995, by Julian Russell, who at that time was an Aikido Shodan Yudansha at the London Aikido Club.

Aikido Journal – 1995
Vol. 22, no. 2

Aikido as a Way of Learning

Julian Russell

Articles in *Aikido Journal* usually focus on the technical aspects or history of Aikido, rather than the "inner" aspects of the art. I imagine that this is because an essential component of the depth of aikido is that it is non-verbal. I have heard my teacher, Andy Hathaway, say that all we have to do is to follow the path that O-Sensei has given us – everything is on this path, all we have to do is to look more deeply into the techniques.

Nevertheless, these thoughts were an important revelation to me when I first heard them. I have also found that a psychological model concerned with the nature of learning has helped me understand some of the richness that I experience in the dojo. I therefore take this opportunity to offer it to other aikidoka in the hope that they may find it of interest. The ideas themselves will not be new to aikidoka, but I believe that this simple way of organizing the ideas may appeal to some.

The model is called "Logical Levels of Learning" or "Learning I, II & III" and comes from the work of Gregory Bateson. "Learning I" takes place when we study the techniques of aikido – *ikkyo*, *nikyo* and the rest in the usual way. "Learning II" takes place when, with time, we learn how to learn aikido more effectively. "Learning III" takes place when we learn about (the purpose of) learning to learn.

Let us look at each level of learning in more detail: "Learning I" is the easiest type to understand. It is what we do when we study the techniques of aikido in increasing detail. During a class, we watch a technique being demonstrated, we attempt to copy what we have seen, and sometimes we get coaching on our particular problems. It seems that we can always examine the technique in greater detail. Even after 20 years or more, you can observe a serious aikidoka still looking more deeply into his technique.

Right at the heart of aikido is the principle of achieving continuous improvement (kaizen) in our techniques – never being satisfied and always looking for further refinements.

Learning to make continuous improvements in our technique is "Learning II" – learning how to learn. The aikido syllabus is so deep that in the process of studying it, students learn to improve the way that they learn. In my own limited experience of aikido, I have attempted to improve my ability to learn aikido in the following ways: keeping my eyes open when the sensei is doing a demonstration and trying to see a new level of detail, rather than saying "I know that one"; listening to what the sensei says rather than getting distracted by other thoughts; remembering the particular point that the sensei made and working specifically on that, especially when the sensei has taken time to give me personal coaching; reducing the number of times I have to be told the same thing by the sensei before it becomes a habit in my body; discovering the similarities between the techniques – *angles*, *hips*, *timing*, *kokyu*, *irimi* and *tenkan* and the subtle interplay between these (this element of learning is known as "pattern recognition"); learning to ignore the feelings of triumph when I think I am doing well and of despair at my physical incompetence when I am doing badly; discovering that if I face things that I find difficult for long enough, I will eventually overcome them; beginning to learn to train irrespective of my whim or mood; learning that natural talent is less important than the number of hours per week on the mat. This is only the personal list of someone relatively new to aikido – I simply offer it as a way of inviting readers' own thoughts about what they have learned about learning.

"Learning III" takes place when we have discovered a new insight about the purpose of learning how to learn (learning about learning to learn). "Learning III" is hard to talk about without sounding pretentious or "spiritual." It is concerned with such questions as the meaning of "learning how to learn," "why bother learning to learn?" or "what is life all about?" As we have discussed, part of the beauty of aikido is that these questions are all handled non-verbally through physical movement – we can explore these questions without words. In "Learning III" words are usually inadequate to describe the experience, and often seem to make little difference to the wisdom, peace of mind, or happiness of the listener.

I will therefore keep my description of "Learning III" to a minimum, simply aiming to inspire readers to notice their own insights.

Obviously Aikido is a microcosm of life itself: we explore the relationship of our own body-mind to the world through the five senses of sight, sound, sensation, smell and taste. We explore our relationship with others through the roles of *uke* and *tori*. We train with a community of people in our dojo.

One way to explore this relationship with life is to ask two questions that paraphrase questions from the Bible: "What is the nature of man, that he should do aikido? What is the nature of aikido, that man should do it?" Stated more personally, I can ask, "What is my nature, that I should do aikido? What is the nature of aikido, that I should do it?"

When Isadora Duncan, a famous dancer, was asked the meaning of a particular dance, she replied "If I could describe it with words, I wouldn't have to dance it."

In speculating on what O-Sensei's reply might have been to a question on the "meaning" of Aikido, we can simply note that in leaving his legacy to the world, O-Sensei left few words but instead cut through our modern world with the sword of his spirit, offering the path of aiki.

Returning to the theme of "Learning I, II and III," it has been helpful to me to understand that I am learning these martial techniques (Learning I) not only for them, but also to learn how to develop myself (Learning II) and perhaps, in the process, learning something about the nature of life (Learning III).

Julian Russell was a nidan student at the London Aikido Club, England. In his professional life he runs courses on personal development and leadership, using a methodology known as Neuro-Linguistic Programming. (www.ppdconsulting.com)

It is often said that in the Martial Arts we have to "steal information", an idea from the "old school" Japanese culture, in order to learn. If we drip feed information to students then we are encouraging, as Psychologist

Martin Seligman calls it; "learned helplessness" and students then get to rely on that constant input.

The Hunter-Gatherer children are "stealing" information from the adults by watching and doing. What strategies do you have for learning and learning how to learn?

In NLP we have the same idea. At some point we have to take responsibility for our own learning. Some Sensei may demonstrate a technique only once or twice and if you are not ready and alert with your eyes on him or her and your ears tuned in you may miss the demonstration.

Remember from Julian Russell's article this is the nature of learning level ll, how to learn so we can be proactive about our own learning and this requires us to be alert, quiet on the inside and present.

THINKING ABOUT THINKING

In the early days of NLP Bandler & Grinder discovered that a lot, if not all therapies available at that time, went after information about the problem. So for instance, those people with phobias and/or past traumas were asked for information about the issue and in order for someone to access that information they will make internal pictures, sounds, feelings, smells and tastes of the experience, (memories) and this will cause them to begin to get physical symptoms, such as increased heart rate, rapid breathing and sweaty palms, as if you were experiencing the stimulus again.

This is also basically the structure of PTSD (Post Traumatic Stress Disorder) when a person can't stop remembering and re-living a past event in vivid detail.

Some therapies actually re-expose the client over and over to the cause of their phobia or trauma over a period of time until they are "de-sensitised". Scary stuff especially if someone is allergic to something.

Richard Bandler didn't see the point in taking the client through more pain so he decided to work with people who had spontaneously changed their own phobias so that he could model what they did and discover their successful strategies.

Why go after more information about the problem, which caused distress, better to study those who had already changed the problem and find out exactly how they had done that.

He advertised in the local press in California offering to pay anyone who had managed to change their phobia to come in and allow themselves to be modelled.

Once Richard had found out how they were doing that and they pretty much all did the same things, he designed a process known as the NLP fast phobia cure and it does exactly what it says, changes a phobia fast and mostly in one session without causing the client to be re-exposed to the stimulus that caused the phobic symptoms.

This is also an example of Einstein's idea:

"You can't solve a problem from the same level or sort of thinking that created it"

Problem solving is what is known as "away from" thinking and is very useful for spotting problems, health & safety, assessing risk and for solving those problems it is also useful to be able to employ a different way of thinking, a "towards" thinking style where you are focused on the goal or solution. Perhaps this is the origin of the phrase: "Thinking out of the Box."

According to neuropsychologist, Dr Rick Hanson, in his book called, "Hardwiring Happiness", human beings' brains have a negativity bias that has evolved over millions of years. People needed to notice dangers from predators and other things such as starvation and other groups of people as this would help to keep them alive much more effectively than only noticing any benefits around them. One mistake and they were dead.

Consequently today this pattern is hardwired and even if we receive positive feedback if there is something negative in it that is what we will zoom in on. We have to work very hard at focussing on and emphasising the positive aspects in our lives and Dr Hanson says we need at least 3 positives to overcome any negativity and to hold those positive feelings for a minimum of 10 seconds.

The point of all this is when confronted with a problem and you are stuck, change your thinking style and look for examples, possibly in other contexts, that work and find out what they are doing and then apply those principles to your own situation.

So we have two ways of thinking or motivating ourselves. Avoiding dangers or problems which is called "Moving Away From" and looking for positives and focussing on achieving goals which is called "Moving Towards". It can be useful to use both styles of thinking as that gives you leverage but if you never consider what you want then you may well end up somewhere you don't want. If you don't know what you want then there are plenty of people who will decide that for you.

In relation to solving problems and being able to achieve what you want, the NLP question is:

"What's stopping you?

And

"What do you want instead?"

This directs us towards a goal and stops us getting bogged down in the problem. You can continue to ask these two questions until you get to a place where you can take action.

This is one of the difficulties with people who want to "stop smoking". When you ask them what their goal is they will say to "stop smoking" or to be a non-smoker and coaching them to also think about what they want instead will enable them to come up with a goal that doesn't remind them of smoking.

It could be something like "to be a healthy person with more energy" so they are immediately seeing different pictures in their minds of themselves in their future.

The Samurai definitely came under the category of "moving away". They spent a lot of time considering the consequences of things going wrong and examining the "worse case scenario".

According to Johnson and Leach, the people who survive in crisis situations are the sort of people who prepare for the worst and practice ahead of time. These people don't deliberate during calamity because they've already done the deliberation the other people around them are just now going through.

In plane crashes, for example, people who have followed the instructions of what to do in an emergency are usually the ones to get out first and survive as they have already noted where the exits are and don't have to think about what to do.

A friend and colleague, Simon Horton, when he was teaching a group about visualisation techniques, used to tell a story about what happened to him on a diving holiday. He was a trained scuba diver but had not dived for some years when he went on holiday with some friends to Mexico to do some diving. On the plane over he thought that as he had not dived for sometime, he would go through the operating and safety procedures of the equipment in his mind, reminding him where everything was and by visualising being in the water and what to do if something were to go wrong.

On one of the dives the air hose broke free from the regulator and bubbles of air suddenly surrounded him as it escaped under pressure from his tank into the water making it difficult for him to see anything. He knew that this was potentially a panic moment. The mouthpiece was still in his mouth so initially the brain thinks it is OK to continue to breathe and obviously it is now water he is breathing in to his lungs.

He quickly looked around for his "Buddy" but then remembered he hadn't been given one and he realised that the nearest person was too far away and the surface was too far up to reach in time. This all happened in seconds and at that moment he remembered there was a spare clip to fix the air hose onto the mouthpiece and he quickly managed to do this.

Later he said that he was convinced his visualising the diving equipment and emergency procedures while on the plane had saved his life.

There is a NLP process that Simon used to teach his students about visualising called The New Behaviour Generator. John Grinder set out the steps to this process in the late 1970s and it is a strategy for generating change in your own behaviour and it can be used for creating completely new behaviours or for making changes to a behaviour you already have and want to change and/or improve.

This process involves you visualising to build up an internal representation, in the three main sensory systems of visual, auditory and kinaesthetic, the new behaviour you want. It works because the unconscious mind has no way of telling the difference between a 'real' event, and something you imagine vividly. You are wiring in a new neural pathway. Later in the book I will tell you about the research of Dr. Blaslotto at the University of Chicago in relation to research about the effectiveness and benefits of visualisation.

Eric Anders emphasises the importance of creating a visual representation of what we are attempting to learn and this takes consistent practice.

Here are the steps to

The New Behaviour Generator

- State your goal in the positive.

- Visualise yourself achieving the goal - this is like you being the director of your own movie so you can make all necessary adjustments and see your self, having already sorted out any problems or difficulties, and now achieving and having your goal and how desirable, attractive and compelling that looks.

    "In the province of the mind, there are no limitations."
    -Dr John Lilly

- When you are satisfied with your desired picture step into the visualisation

- **Ask** yourself if it **feels** like you can actually do it

- State what is needed or missing and step out again to make those changes to your visualisation and step into the picture to check again

Research shows the most powerful way to combat stress or anxiety is to stay calm and to have a feeling of control. For Samurai, training tirelessly and visualizing the worst that could happen gave them a feeling of control while in battle.

Anything that increases your perception of control over a situation, whether it actually increases your control or not, can substantially decrease your stress level.

Build yourself a daily practice of generating new behaviours by visualising you doing them now.

Aikido is considered by many to be "Self Defence" which implies we wait until attacked. This is a misunderstanding that ignores the "Awase" element and gives the initiative and control to the attacker. If I give an opening that determines how someone approaches or attacks me, who is attacking who? Any opening is bait.

"All warfare is based on deception" – The Art of War, Sun Tzu

Another example of taking control of a difficult situation is where many businesses are finding it difficult to make a profit or even survive in the current economic meltdown. However, even in the tough economic times, there are some organisations that are reporting up to 24% improvement in their profits. This is the idea of "isomorphism": looking for areas where there are the needed resources and then moving these resources into the problem context.

The NLP way is to model that success and apply the strategies those successful individuals or groups are using, to their own situations. I found out that the answer to this little mystery is to invest in "Customer Care Training" so that your customers or clients enjoy their experience, come back repeatedly and tell their friends about the good service. They become marketeers on behalf of your business.

When people decide to use your business and services make sure they want to come back for more. One of my sons has a USP (unique selling point) for his building design business of high quality in his work and will always do something extra, (for free) that the client hasn't asked for. This way he gets a lot of repeat business and new clients who are referred by satisfied customers.

CHANGING BAD MEMORIES

Having self awareness and some knowledge of the representational system or VAKOG also means we can utilise the ability to make adjustments to how we are thinking in order to deal with past traumas and difficulties as well as building internal pictures of compelling futures.

When you recall past experiences you are not actually dealing with the original event but rather your current perception of it, i.e. a memory and this is in your thinking, probably an internal picture, and therefore you can adjust your thinking in the present to deal with any issues from the past and you don't actually need to delve into the original cause.

A good example of this is when someone who has a phobia or an allergy will get physical symptoms such as increased heart rate, rapid breathing and sweaty hands just by thinking about the thing they are afraid of or by thinking about the substance they are allergic to.

I am amazed at seeing TV news broadcasts of trauma victims being asked by journalists to describe the traumatic event and how they feel about it and as they do so they are re-associating the victim back into the trauma state of fear and panic and, just as in the exercise we did earlier, they display the non-verbal signals of trauma and are, more often than not, left in a tearful state. I think it would be a good idea to offer some training to people in those situations so that they know how to leave their interviewees in a good or at least neutral state when they have finished the interview.

It is a prerequisite that a NLP Coach leave their client in at least as good as, if not better state, than they found them in and I think this would be a good principle for media people in general to aspire to.

One strategy that could be used would be to ask the person to look back and see their selves in the memory rather than be back in it, associated in the feelings as if it was happening again. That way they wouldn't re-experience the feelings but it needs the ability to calibrate their non verbal signals and careful managing of their state.

NLP has ways to change how someone thinks that creates their fear or how their immune system is generalising to create an allergy and this can usually be done in one or over a few sessions.

One of the things Richard Bandler often says is:

"The best thing about the past is that it is over".

"We do not heal the past by dwelling there; we heal the past by living fully in the present". – Marianne Williamson

We can do the same thing with our goals. Think of something you want, make a vivid, colourful picture of yourself achieving that goal in your mind, now experience the good feeling you get when you do this.

Now increase the size, colour, and movement of this internal picture and bring it closer and notice how the good feeling you get from having already achieved your goal intensifies as you make these adjustments.

Some people might say that they are not able to visualise and if that were true they would not be able to remember their friends. Think about a family member or friend and you will probably make an internal picture of them and/or hear their voice. This normally happens automatically and slightly out of conscious awareness and now that I have brought it to your conscious attention you can begin to notice what's going on inside for you.

Internal pictures are not the same as we see on the outside, that would be concerning if it was the case. They can be faint and almost imperceptible and for some people they are extremely vivid. I had a friend, an Oxford Maths Graduate who could visualise so well that she could do equations on the inside in her head and was surprised when she discovered that I and most other people just couldn't do that.

The way to improve your visualisation abilities is to keep practising. Recall a face or whole body or an object. What happens if you rotate the object or make it bigger or smaller?

Being able to visualise your memories means you can visualise someone demonstrating a physical skill and see yourself successfully performing that skill. You can also make adjustments to reduce or clear unwanted baggage and to make goals even more attractive and also ways to get yourself motivated.

The brain can't tell the difference between something real or imagined. When you mentally rehearse and build your new habits, you are literally building new neural pathways and you strengthen your ability to create them in your life.

Identify images that align with accomplishing your goal and spend time visualising them daily.

If you have annoying internal pictures (memories) that cause you to have unpleasant feelings and you want to change them, make sure you have all the useful information and learning from that event and then change the pictures to black and white, shrink them down smaller and smaller, blink them on and off, on and off and send them into the distance and over the horizon. This will reduce the intensity of any feelings or remove them entirely. It is also very useful to immediately and at the same time as you reduce the picture of that memory that you had, replace that image with a vivid picture of you without those negative feelings and achieving what you want instead.

Repeat this process about five times and you will have wired in a new pathway and the brain will automatically choose that direction every time you think about that memory, getting you to more positive and useful feelings.

Walt Disney was interviewed outside a cinema having just watched the premiere of his latest film. A journalist asked him what his next project was and Walt replied that he didn't know yet but what he did know was that whatever it was it would be big, bright and colourful.

CHAPTER 4 –
THE PRESUPPOSITIONS OF NLP

"Modelling is the heart of NLP and the Presuppositions are the spirit."
– Judy Delozier

I wonder if the Presuppositions are also the equivalent of "kokyu" in Aikido. One of the meanings of kokyu is "breath" which I think is pretty close to spirit. They say that without "kokyu" it is not Aikido and certainly without operating out of the Presuppositions it is not NLP. It would be like the breath of life had gone out of it and it had no spirit.

The core principles of NLP are called "The Presuppositions" and like all NLP they come from various fields via the process of modelling an excellent or successful piece of behaviour and it is useful to consider some of them.

I haven't seen a more comprehensive explanation of the Presuppositions than written by Judith DeLozier and Robert Dilts in the NLP Encyclopaedia:

http://nlpuniversitypress.com/html2/PrPu23.html

http://nlpuniversitypress.com/html2/PrPu24.html

Here's a brief introduction to some of the Presuppositions:

> **"The meaning of your communication is the response you get."**

This refers directly to the communication loop and flips normal thinking on its head, and puts the responsibility on the person sending the communication to make sure it lands. You're the one sending the communication, so you have to start watching and listening to the response of your customers, clients, students, friends etc to know whether they have heard and understood the meaning of what you're saying!

Some people, for instance, will continually speak to others very quietly or mumble and speak very fast and as a consequence of that the person they are speaking to will be constantly saying pardon, sorry I didn't hear that and leaning forward to try and get closer and hear better. Often the listener will give up after a while and stop trying to hear and understand.

Anyone who wants to be able to communicate effectively needs to notice and hear the responses from the listener. When you see someone leaning forward, straining to hear what you have said, that is his or her response to your communication.

They can't hear you. Speak up.

"The single biggest problem in communication is the illusion that it has taken place" – George Bernard Shaw

The Communication Loop

When you learn to live this presupposition it has the ability to change how well you communicate with others. It takes you out of the blame frame and puts you in a position to communicate and influence with integrity. Carl Rogers who created the field of Person Centered Therapy said that the only person who can't be helped is that person who blames others.

Consider a learning/teaching context. A student says:

"I don't understand this."

The Teacher now has a choice to blame the student.

E. G. "Well I've told you how it works. You should listen."

The Teacher assumes the student has not learnt because he/she is not listening and the student is left not knowing and probably feeling bad. The Teacher is frustrated and neither of them has gained from the interaction.

It is much more useful and productive for the teacher to accept that the student has not understood and then deliver the information in a different way. The teacher's thought and possible reply might then be:

"OK so you don't understand, yet, so let's go through it again and this time I'll show and tell you in a different way".

The teacher can utilise many different strategies for delivering information until the student is able to understand. The more strategies the teacher has the more effective the student's learning. A good teacher will understand the principle of information overload, the use of metaphor in the teaching and learning process (as in this book), when and how to switch to **more right brain activities** and the importance of "chunking".

Also a teacher has the ability to monitor and help manage a student's state so they are even more able to learn. Both the teacher and the student will gain from these interactions.

This presupposition is also very useful, if not essential, in relationships.

Another of the NLP Presuppositions states:

"The Map is not the Territory"

People respond to their own perceptions of reality and every person has his or her own representation or map of the world. No individual map of the world is any more "real" or "true" than any other. All maps have some validity and all maps delete information.

This goes back to how we use our senses to gather information, process, and store and recall it and we do that in different ways depending on the sensory channel(s) we prefer. This difference in itself can cause a lot of communication problems, particularly in relationships, because people will use different words when operating out of their own particular map.

For instance someone may be talking about feeling and getting a sense of something while another person may describe it by seeing or looking and it is as if they are speaking a different language.

Some people have strong maps and talk about "the right thing" to do and are unaware they are trying to impose their own maps on others, often in the guise of helping. In other words they want others to be like them because it's "the right thing to do" or they have no experience of someone else's map.

"Right for whom?" I say, and "Who said so?"

When someone talks about the "right thing", a judgement is being made.

Better to ask: "Is it useful and does it work?"

It's very important to be aware of this when modelling to avoid making your own meanings and assumptions about what someone is doing.

Nan-in, a Japanese Zen master during the Meiji era, received a university professor who came to inquire about Zen.

Nan-in served tea. He poured his visitor's cup full, and then kept on pouring. The professor watched the overflow until he no longer could restrain himself. "It is overfull. No more will go in!"

"Like this cup", Nan-in said, "You are full of your own opinions and speculations. How can I show you Zen unless you first empty your cup?"

A mind full of conclusions has no room for expansion.

The most effective and ecological maps or models of the world are those that make available the widest and richest number of choices, as opposed to being the most "right", "real" or "accurate".

We all have our own beliefs and it is generally not possible to persuade someone verbally to change their belief. There are some beliefs we have learnt as children which will change naturally as we acquire more information.

A belief is only a belief, a generalisation that we are taking to be true all the time and in all situations. It is not "The Truth" or "Reality". It is made up of a set of values, meanings that can motivate us in powerful ways or limit us just as powerfully by way of behaviours, skills and permissions. They are a product of our programming, intellectual backfill, as John Grinder said.

For example:

At the level of behaviour and capability: -

I can't… I am not allowed to…

I don't know how or what to do

I don't have the necessary skills or know how to get them.

Put the emphasis on the "I" and they also become beliefs about identity, about who we are.

Some other beliefs at the level of identity: –

I am not good enough

I am not worth it

I don't deserve it

I am not that sort of person

People like us can/can't…

These are particularly powerful beliefs about our selves and are often formed in the first 5 or 6 years of life. You can see and understand that by having beliefs opposite to some of these will have a powerful effect in a positive way about how we perceive ourselves. As a coach for 25 years it is mostly these beliefs that people have about themselves that I have had to help them deal with.

What is going on in the Middle East is a classic example of "right mapping" and imposing that map on others in the most extreme ways. All religion is a belief system and no one of them is more real or true than any other. It is simply a belief and it is ironic that some religious people who preach that we should love each other will fight and die in defence of their beliefs and will kill anyone who disagrees with them.

Perhaps wisdom and the possibility to move forward comes from the ability to sit down with others and discuss your differences without the need to change them and maybe this sort of thinking can be the salvation of the human race, should it ever choose to look and go for a solution as opposed to "being right".

Another Presupposition states:

"If you always do what you've always done you will always get the same result"

If what you are doing is not working and you are not achieving your outcome, do something different to get a different result.

Saito Sensei used to say when he was teaching: *"Zero plus zero equals zero"* or as my father used to say, *"Two wrongs don't make a right."*

This could be a good one for Bankers and Governments to consider, e.g. bombing doesn't always work, doesn't solve the problem, and it usually kills even more people, causing more bitterness and blame. A severe economic crash is created by questionable methods motivated by an expectation of excessive profits, in other words, greed. Slowly the economy recovers and making profits once again creates fear and greed that motivates people and another crash looms.

"Insanity is doing the same thing over and over and expecting a different result".

This quote is often attributed to Einstein and it is a bit like banging your head against a brick wall. It's nice when you stop. I said that.

In both Aikido and NLP we feel the "bump" of conflict when there is disagreement or we meet strength with strength and in order to move forward you need to make some sort of adjustment in what you are doing like "get off the centre line". Later in this book you will learn how to do this in any situation, just like the old man in the train.

"There is no such thing as failure only feedback, information and renewed opportunities"

"Failure is the key to success; each mistake teaches us something"
– The Art of Peace, O Sensei

A lot of innovations have come about by bringing together diverse ideas from different fields and then trialling the result, fixing and adjusting errors and trying again. This process of learning and fixing "failures" and retesting is more efficient than spending lots of time theorising until the "perfect result" may be discovered.

Maybe we could all benefit from having our own "Black Box" and addressing mistakes, errors and failures so that you can learn in an on-going way. This is what we get when training in Aikido, constant feedback. We are making mistakes all the time because the techniques are not yet wired in and the feedback enables you to adjust what you are doing.

This is known as an "Open Loop". A "Closed Loop" is where mistakes are not addressed and investigated and this prevents any learning. The Airline Industry and the Health Service are two examples of differing values around "failures". Hopefully this is changing in the Health Services now.

Matthew Syed talks about "marginal improvements" and says in his book: "Black Box Thinking" that:

"Learning from mistakes relies on two things: you need to have a system that harnesses errors as a means of driving progress; and second you need a mind-set that enables such a system to flourish."

Aikido requires this process of constantly addressing our errors and this can be a difficulty for those students who consider feedback as criticism at the level of identity, about who they are and then go into negative states and beat themselves up.

"Many of life's failures are people who did not realize how close they were to success when they gave up." – Thomas Edison: American inventor and businessman

John Sculley of Apple said: *"If you aren't making mistakes, you aren't trying hard enough."*

In Aikido this is known as "Awase", where and when we hit a "bump in the landscape", as Judy Delozier describes it, then you need to adjust what you are doing in order to blend with the person's energy and momentum, get around their strength without struggle by finding the path of no resistance and be able to effect them in a useful way which would primarily be by taking their center, balance and spirit.

Andy Hathaway Sensei often quotes Saito Shihan who said that there was no such thing as a mistake or wrong technique because there will always be another possibility and the skill is being able to continue to blend and maintain the connection and keep them off balance, in order to lead. These are the priorities rather than a technique. This is known as Pacing in NLP. Metaphorically walking at the same pace as the other person will build rapport and then you are able to lead (influence) them.

"In improvisation, there are no mistakes. If you hit a wrong note, it's the next note that you play that determines if it's good or bad.

It's always been a gift with me hearing music the way I do. I don't know where it comes from; its just there and I don't question it." – Miles Davis

Verbal pacing is saying what you know to be true in the world for the other person at that time so if they say something like,

"This is difficult" you could pace them by replying, "Yes it is difficult" or "Yes it can be difficult".

You could then put in a lead such as: "And here's a little trick that will help and you'll be surprised at how quickly you can begin to learn how to do this even better as you continue to persevere". This last piece is known as "future pacing", basically connecting the present situation to what is possible in the future in a positive way.

Without the acknowledgement of "yes it can be difficult" the reply becomes a mismatch to that person's experience, the relationship is not enhanced and communication and learning becomes difficult.

Often a persons' initial response might be to deny the difficulty and offer a solution, e.g.

"No it's not difficult, why don't you do this?"

All well intended but this is a mismatch, nevertheless.

Actually I have already introduced a lead in my second answer. By inserting the words, "can be", I have implied that sometimes it might not be difficult and this will often by-pass a person's conscious mind and we have then introduced the idea of "possibility" instead of difficulty. If the person does not accept this, we then go back to pacing some more.

Pacing, pacing and then leading and if the person doesn't follow go back to pacing some more and then lead them again and repeat this until they do follow.

This is: **The Structure of Influence.**

You are leading or influencing them with integrity because you are helping them into a more positive state of "possibility" which means they are more able to deal with what was a "difficulty".

When someone codes feedback as failure or criticism they tend to defend themselves, go into a negative state and this will often hold him or her back from considering the feedback, learning from it and then moving forwards.

Josh Waitzkin who is a Chess Grand Master and Tai Chi Push Hands World Champion says he doesn't really remember his successes but rather his failures, all the times he lost matches because that is where he will learn the most and learning is what he is most excited about.

Some people will be given feedback at the level of identity and interpret that feedback as being about who they are rather than what they are doing, feel bad and give up.

I was one of those people and it was painful. I learnt to pause and say:

"Oh that's interesting, I really screwed up there" and crucially, "I wonder what I did so wrong and how can I change it?"

Training in the Dojo, on the mat, we are constantly being corrected. That is the nature of learning Aikido or anything else for that matter and some people may find this difficult to deal with because they code those corrections as criticism and that causes them to feel bad and come up with reasons to defend themselves.

The worst thing that can happen to a student is to be ignored.

"A person does not exist until they are seen and blessed" – Albert Camus

Of course, as we have discussed, how we deliver that feedback is very important and will make a difference to how it is received. Both sides of the communication loop contribute to the learning experience.

Pacing or building rapport can be done by matching the others physiology including their breathing, their language, values and beliefs etc. We don't have to take on their beliefs, just acknowledge that they have that belief, which is pacing. A belief is not the "truth" or "reality", it is simply a belief, however miss-matching at the level of belief causes conflict so it is very important to use pacing. People will fight and die over their beliefs, just take a look around the world at the many conflicts and they are usually caused by beliefs about religion, territory and resources.

When I first learnt about pacing peoples experience an opportunity to try it out arose one day when I was out with my young sons in a busy shopping area on a Saturday afternoon in London.

One of the things young children want to do as soon as they can walk is to be able to run. They can quickly learn to do this but being able to stop and keep their balance is another thing and often they fall over and cut or scrape their knees.

You may have had the experience of witnessing this happening, the child is on the ground, hurting and crying and the parent hurries over and says.

"Don't cry it doesn't hurt".

Put yourself in the child's position. It does hurt; they may be bleeding and might also be frightened. This is confusing for the child, is a mismatch because their experience is not being acknowledged and their crying and fear may escalate.

Now the parent's intention is not to escalate the situation but rather to comfort the child, (positive intention). However, how the child feels right then is not being acknowledged and they may well cry more.

When this happened with my son I went up to him, got down to his level and said.

"Wow you have fallen over and cut your knee which probably hurts. Look at how red your blood is, that is really good blood. Do you think it needs a bandage or a plaster?"

He stopped crying and replied that it needed a plaster, got up, took my hand and we headed to the nearest shop to buy some plasters.

What I did was to pace his experience and this had an effect on how he was feeling. His experience was being acknowledged. "Yes it did hurt". It hadn't been my intention to stop him crying but that is what happened.

The other thing my question did, after I had paced him, was to switch him from the feeling system, pain and fear, and direct him to the visual system by saying "Look at how red his blood was" and choosing between a bandage and plaster meant he was thinking ahead and was also involved and had some control over his own healing.

This is an example of pacing and leading. Energy flows where attention goes.

Verbal pacing is saying what you know to be true for that person in the world at that time. Use their words or at least some of them when pacing back what they have said.

Pacing or blending and connecting In Aikido is called Awase and is in all techniques and paired Boken (wooden sword) and Jo (wooden staff) work and constant practise is required for excellent performance of technique. We need to respond in the same time that any attack is happening.

Move too early and the other person has time to adjust.

Chapter 5 – Awareness

Awareness and self-awareness can also be thought of as "Mindfulness"

When O Sensei died in 1968 he left his Dojo (Practice Hall) in Iwama to his long-term student Morihei Saito Sensei who was once interviewed by Stanley Pranin, the editor of Aiki Journal magazine who subsequently printed a story about Saito Sensei and the local Yakusa (Japanese Mafia) in Iwama.

There had been a dispute between the Yakusa and some of Saito Sensei's young Aikido students and a confrontation had been arranged one evening in the street, a bit like a scene from the movie "High Noon".

Saito Sensei heard about this and decided to go along. He walked down the street flanked by his students and stopped opposite the local Yakusa Boss who was accompanied by his henchmen.

After a pause Saito Sensei bowed to the Yakusa boss and said:

"I want to apologise for the behaviour of my students. I haven't taught them well enough yet and they still have a lot to learn."

He then turned to his students and ordered them into the nearest bar to buy drinks for all the Yakusa. Honour was restored and there was never any conflict between the groups again.

Saito Sensei took responsibility for teaching his students and knew that they had not yet got the concept of non-conflict (awase) outside the dojo and needed continued tuition and training. Learning to manage themselves was just as important as martial art techniques.

Saito Sensei's behaviour in this situation was a demonstration to his students of how to deal with conflict and in NLP terms he was pacing or acknowledging what he knew to be true for the others.

For some people letting go of "being right" is difficult but it's simply a way of achieving what you want when you have the courage and curiosity to step into another person's map of the world.

Imagine applying these principles in life in general or in Israel, Palestine, Afghanistan and now Syria etc. It's so simple and so radical compared to what is going on now which is escalation of an already disastrous situation. They are trapped in their own maps and fighting in defence of their own beliefs.

"Men do not learn a lot from the lessons of history and that is the most important lesson of history" – Aldous Huxley

Governments, many people, operate out of their own maps, assume their map is the best or right one and try to impose it on others thus creating conflict. Of course there will be some people who like to be directed and will follow. Anyone with a strong map can do this imposing without being aware of what they are doing simply because they have such a strong map its hard for them to be aware of other peoples' maps and different ways to do things.

It's a bit like asking a fish how the water is. The fish is so used to being in that environment it doesn't know what water is and is not aware that another environment exists that is different and that there may be other resources there.

Musashi believed that there is a level of understanding of life that could be reached whereby one became invincible. He said:

"I am invincible because I offer no resistance".

This is what we do in NLP and on the mat in Aikido. Pacing someone literally takes the wind out of their sails and there is nothing for them to "fight" against. What you resist persists. When someone is obviously angry we can pace him or her by saying something like: "I can see and hear you feel strongly about this." They obviously do because they are probably being loud and emotional which indicates they have strong feelings about something. Remember only say what you know to be true, what do you specifically see and hear the other person doing and saying.

This takes practise and is an amazing place to be. We take one step outside the situation and monitor the process without being judgemental, for the purpose of getting to some sort of solution or at least keeping the momentum going in a useful direction. Practise with a friend or colleague and just feedback one sentence and wait and see what happens.

We are so wired to put forward our own ideas, meanings and solutions that it can be a phenomenal realisation and discovery that we can do so much more with less. Any conflict tends to drag us into defending ourselves and blaming others, which in turn elicits emotions that takes us into a less than useful loop or spiral and uses a lot of emotional energy.

An example of this is a time I went to watch one of my sons play football (soccer). He plays in midfield in front of the defenders and behind the strikers and during the first half of the game he was constantly being harangued by one of the defenders on his team behind him.

This particular defender kept barking out orders for him to go and mark someone, watch that gap or pass the ball more quickly and I could see my son's physiology changing to his "pissed off" mode. As they came off for the halftime break he was obviously angry and his team were 2 goals down.

After a while when he had got his drink he wandered over to where I was standing on the touchline and a few of his mates came with him.

He asked me if I had seen and heard that "expletive defender" and if he started shouting at him in the second half my son said he would chin him.

They stood in a huddle looking at me and eventually I said:

"Yes he's just as passionate as you at wanting to win this game, isn't he?"

They all stood there watching me, not saying a word and then the ref blew his whistle for the second half and they turned and ran onto the field.

Well they were like a different team in the second half and ended up winning the game 3 – 2.

What my son had experienced in the first half caused him to feel anxious and angry. The meaning he made of his teammate shouting at him was one of being criticized and those feelings of anxiety and anger had rippled through the team so they were not in a high performance state and were being beaten. What I had done was rather than criticise the defender's behaviour I paced his probable positive intention of being passionate about wanting to win. He obviously cared about something.

I had relabelled or reframed the meaning of his "criticism" as one of communication and wanting to win and that meant they were all aligned as a team, in a better performance state and focused on beating the other team. Now when they heard the defender barking out orders it meant he was communicating rather than criticising and they were glad he was there, literally covering their backs, an extra pair of eyes, reminding and encouraging them.

I am often aware of this when watching professional football teams playing. They can be elite athletes and yet sometimes look awkward and lacking confidence. One small simple input like the one above can make the difference. Suddenly they look relaxed and are playing as a team.

Awareness

There is a scene in the movie "Seven Samurai" where a young new recruit is being interviewed to join a small group of warriors who are hired to defend a village with only food for payment, from an army of bandits and the young man is a bit of an imposter, a wannabe Samurai. The Master Swordsman sets up a welcoming test and places a warrior inside the doorway out of sight and holding a wooden stick poised ready to strike.

The young imposter stepped through the doorway and was immediately hit with the stick sending him crashing to the floor. He was unaware that someone was hiding inside the doorway waiting to hit him. When the same test had been made of the Master Swordsman he avoided the strike and nearly killed the attacker with one swift move.

He knew even before the strike came that there was danger. His awareness and sensitivity of others came from martial art training. The best technique in the world is no good if you are not aware of other potential dangers of attack. One of the instructions constantly heard in an Iwama Ryu Aikido Dojo is:

"Keep your head up. Where are the others?"

Budo is a Japanese word, which roughly translated means "fighting spirit", and the Samurai would say:

"It is bad Budo to get into a fight. It means that you have not seen, heard or sensed it coming".

This awareness is also an important part of NLP training and is known as "calibration of non verbal signals". I was having a drink with a group of Aikidoka after training one night, in an Irish pub down the road from the Dojo. We were sitting as a group in a corner near the door and I was perched on a stool near the way out.

Suddenly I had this overwhelming compulsion to move. Even though I was engaged in conversation I had to move and found myself standing up with a pint in my hand and everyone staring at me and wondering what I was doing. I sat down in a different place and just then a scuffle broke out and two men were bundled out through the door right past where I had been sitting.

Later the Landlord of the pub told me they were IRA guys trying to extract protection money from him that they framed as a subscription to the cause. As he told me this I recall hearing him say repeatedly, "Please finish your drinks and leave." I had not registered it consciously at the time but remembered there was something about his tone of voice that had got my attention, albeit mostly out of my conscious awareness, and that was what had alerted my unconscious to potential danger and caused me to move.

You have probably had the experience of asking someone you know well, a question and before they said anything you knew whether their answer was going to be yes or no. Children are very good at doing this and they know just the right moment to ask their parents for something. In fact we are all very good at doing this, particularly with people we know well such as family members, colleagues, friends or lovers.

The question is "**How** do we know this?" We repeatedly see the tiny physical cues that tell us the answer is "yes or no" even before they have said anything. Most of this information is taken in unconsciously and some people might call this intuition and I maintain that intuition, that feeling that guides our decisions and actions, is a result of unconscious calibration and because it happens out of conscious awareness, how we know is by a certain feeling. In NLP this is known as a congruence signal or kinaesthetic check.

Cues like a raised eyebrow, a tensing of muscles at the ends of the mouth, tensing of skin and muscles between the eyes that we call frowning, lips thinning as the blood drains out, skin tone changes as we go "white or pale with fear" or "flushed with success", and a shift of the head back or forwards. My Mother could demonstrate some of these signals as well as a certain tone of voice and I am immediately triggered back to childhood.

All of these tiny cues, and more, happen in different combinations and when put together are a pattern that shows a certain internal state or mood that indicates a positive response or not.

Do this as an exercise sometime in the next few minutes:

- Ask someone to think about a "negative" memory (not the worse thing that has ever happened to them) and you will begin to see non-verbal signals as the person enters the negative state associated with the memory.
- Break their state by talking about something mundane or get them to move around a bit and notice their NVS shifting from the negative state.

- Ask them about a "positive or happy" memory and you will see signals indicating a positive state. These signals may be small but the potential that you have to notice them even more can be learnt surprisingly easily when you consciously practice.

- Ask the questions in that order so you leave the person in a positive state. An example of the power of leading a person's state with a simple question. One of the outcomes of a NLP coach is to always leave the client in a better state than you found them.

You may have come across a quote from O Sensei explaining his idea of what the martial arts are really for:

"The Way of the Warrior has been misunderstood. It is not a means to kill and destroy others. Those who seek to compete and better one another are making a terrible mistake. To smash, injure, or destroy is the worst thing a human being can do. The real Way of a Warrior is to prevent such slaughter – it is the Art of Peace, the power of love." – O Sensei

Just as important as awareness is self-awareness and this can also be thought of as "Mindfulness", the gentle effort to be continuously present.

The Oxford English Dictionary definition of mindfulness is: "the state or quality of being mindful".

Mindfulness is a state of active, open attention on the present. When you're mindful, you observe your thoughts and feelings without judging them good or bad. Instead of letting your life pass you by, mindfulness means living in the moment and awakening to experience.

One of the key skills in an Aikido Dojo is awareness of what is happening around us so we are absorbing non verbal signals and building our awareness about which way somebody is about to move, or noticing if there is room for your partner to fall safely. When I am teaching NLP and want to help students learn the skill of calibrating non-verbal signals, I initially use an exercise demonstrating this, which I call "Baby Left or Baby Right?"

This is based on something English Radio DJ and TV Presenter Chris Evans used to do on his TV programme "TFI Friday." A short piece of film was run which showed a baby that was sitting on a bed and unable to keep its balance it wobbles one way and then the next. This continues and then the film is stopped and the guest on the show was asked to guess which way the baby falls, left or right. Hence the title, "Baby left or baby right."

What I did was utilise this idea and got two people sitting opposite each other, one sets their intention to stand up and move to the left or right and the other person's job is to indicate which way they are going to move as soon as they think they know.

After a few goes a person can learn to recognise which direction their partner is going to move with only the minimal amount of physical movement. Just by setting an intention and deciding which way they are going to move, they will display non-verbal signals, which, with a few practice goes, can be recognised as meaning moving to the left or the right.

I have used this exercise to teach business people about non-verbal signals and they have been amazed at how good they get in such a short time, not realising that they are probably already good at this in certain circumstances, albeit unconsciously. Knowing about it gives them the ability to also use it consciously in any situation.

We unconsciously recognise these patterns of non-verbal behaviour in others once we have seen them demonstrated consistently and in NLP they are very important and are useful indicators of a person's state, intention, and curiosity or not or simply yes or no. In the words of Musashi, *"these should be studied carefully."*

Each person is different and we may need to have seen the cues more than once to learn their meaning. We can make good guesses about what some signals mean and we may be right a lot of the time but we need to be very careful of making meanings about what we think somebody is thinking or feeling.

It is very easy to impose our own maps, ideas and beliefs on others and when we get it wrong we can unwittingly elicit a negative state in someone, lose rapport because it is a mismatch to their experience and so caution is needed. It is best to check by asking the person how they are unless you are already certain.

We can make assumptions and apply meanings about how someone has communicated with us or make meanings about how they look and these may be totally wrong. For instance we could think that a person sitting hunched over and looking down might be depressed whereas they might actually be concentrating on something, like the figure in Rodin's statue, "The Thinker".

As soon as you ask someone if they are upset or depressed they will automatically search for and connect to examples of those states in their history thus eliciting the negative feelings that go along with them.

In the areas of relationships, coaching, teaching, business meetings, sales or potential dangers, non-verbal signals are an important part of the package of excellent and effective communication. When Bandler and Grinder modelled hypnotherapist Milton Erickson, they discovered his amazing ability to read the smallest of non-verbal signals as he observed or talked to his clients.

Dilation of the pupils of a person's eyes would indicate the person was entering an altered or trance state; a slight lightening of skin tone or thinning of the lips could mean a shift into a less than resourceful state. In the early NLP books Bandler and Grinder often said that most information would be displayed non-verbally and all we have to do is pay attention.

There is some doubt as to the validity of the original research entitled "Silent Messages" carried out by Albert Mehrabian and the meaning made by others that says that up to 93% of communication is non-verbal, as this research was specific to attitudes and feelings.

Nevertheless the essence of the model - even when used in overly simplistic form – is powerful and generally helpful, and certainly better than placing undue reliance on words alone for conveying (receiving and sending) communications, especially those which carry potentially emotional implications. In coaching this is very important especially when asking a question.

You need to be watching the other person as you ask the question because their brain is already processing and non-verbal signals are being displayed even before the question is finished. Many people in a variety of contexts will have their heads down and be making notes or tapping away on a computer as they ask the question(s), like my Doctor one time, a locum, thereby missing the non-verbal signals. He never looked at me either while he was asking the questions or when I was answering and kept his eyes on the keyboard. Just think about how much information he was missing.

Sometimes there is too much emphasis on task rather than relationship and In the Dojo it is very important to keep your eyes on the other person and it is all too easy to look down at where you are being held or where you are holding them. The same goes for ken training, instead of looking at the weapon, watch the person, not looking in their eyes but watching the whole person.

When Hypnotherapist, Milton Erickson was a young man he suffered from Polio and was confined to bed and unable to move for about 2 years. His family lived in a house in Phoenix and as the young Milton lay in his bed upstairs listening to the sounds in the house he began to learn who was there by the way they moved and the noises they made.

He could hear the front gate opening and the sounds as a person walked down the path to the front door. Eventually these sounds became like a movie to him and he could tell who had stepped through the front gate long before they reached the front door of the house.

The family also had a new baby and when it began to crawl it was sometimes left in Milton's room and he would lay in bed watching the baby crawl, sit up, grab something and pull itself up onto its shaky legs and feet and fall over many times in its attempts to learn to walk. It was so motivated to do the things that big people could do that it would start again after every fall, make a small adjustment and basically teach itself, literally step by step, to walk.

Milton said later that he copied (modelled) the micro muscle movements from the baby and began to teach himself to be able to move again. He said that he thought if he can learn to move one finger then he could expand this and, as everything is connected, begin to move the rest of his fingers and then his hand and other hand etc.

The baby has no inhibitions and learns by trial and error, feedback systems, determination and perseverance to achieve its goal of walking. By the age of two most of us had already learnt to walk and talk and a lot of that learning you did by modelling the big people around you, just as the hunter/gatherer children do.

Another NLP Presupposition says:

"People already have all the resources they need"

"The divine is not something high above us. It is in heaven, it is in earth, it is inside us." – The Art of Peace, O Sensei

- Individual skills are a function of the development and sequencing of representational systems.

- Since human beings share the same basic representational capabilities, it is possible for any individual to access and organise representations in order to recreate or approach any individual human phenomena. It is thus possible to model and transfer any human capability from one person to another.

- People already have (or potentially have) all of the resources they need to act effectively. Change comes from releasing or triggering the appropriate resource (or activating the potential resource) for a particular context by enriching the individual's model of the world.

The Buddha said: *"Look within, thou art the Buddha."*

Jesus said: *"The kingdom of Heaven is within you."*

This was Musashi's insight as well:

"There is nothing outside of yourself that can ever enable you to get better, stronger, richer, quicker, or smarter. Everything is within. Everything exists. Seek nothing outside of yourself." – Miyamoto Musashi

Dr. Milton Erickson realised that we are hard-wired to learn and the resources to do that are already in our systems. He always presupposed that people already have all the resources they need and he utilised this knowledge in his work with his clients and never considered that they were broken. We always have to accept and start where the "client" is.

He said that: "The problem is the solution". An example of this is how he "tasked" his clients to do something which would eventually lead them to solve their own problem.

Erickson became the Medical Director in a hospital and one day went to visit a long-term resident, a patient who had a delusion that he was Jesus Christ. At that time Erickson was aware there was some building work going on in another part of the hospital and he said to the patient:

"I understand you are a carpenter?"

Now this paced or acknowledged the patient's delusion and also put the patient in a double bind. If he said no he wasn't a carpenter then he could no longer maintain his delusion of being Jesus Christ.

He accepted Erickson's proposition and was sent to work with the builders, who were not going to be very accepting of his delusion, and within 3 months he was released into the community where he successfully worked in the building trade.

A client came to see Erickson about stopping smoking. Erickson asked him how many packs of cigarettes he smoked a day and where he bought them. He then instructed the client to buy only one small pack at a time and to walk to a shop on the other side of town to buy them.

Very soon the client got fed up walking several miles across town every time he wanted a new pack of cigarettes and then walking several miles home and he eventually stopped smoking and of course he had been improving his fitness in the process, found that he liked walking and discovered many interesting areas of the town he had never noticed before.

By asking the client to do this Erickson was pacing their issue and then leading them with his suggestion. This would also bring their conscious attention to an activity that is mostly done out of conscious awareness, i.e. smoking, and you would eventually get to a point of being fed up and sick of "doing that problem". Also walking across town preserved some of the possible benefits of smoking such as:

- Being on your own
- Relaxing
- Taking time out
- Dealing with stress
- Being calm

For younger people the benefits of smoking can also include:

- Being a rebel
- Looking glamorous
- Being strong and grown up

- Being with their friends who smoke, peer pressure, often the reason a person starts smoking

Often a person has an unconscious fear of losing these benefits if they stop smoking or change their behaviour in some way and this can prevent them from taking any action to make that change. In fact I would advise anyone to keep smoking until they find other ways to continue to get those benefits instead of smoking. If you take away their ability to deal with stress and to be calm it may leave them in a less than useful state and may also adversely affect their health.

Some people who are quitting smoking complain about the "craving" they experience and Richard Bandler interprets this as a signal to let you know that you are on the right track.

As a coach or friend it is important to develop a good relationship with the person, pace/acknowledge their concern and reassure them that they won't lose anything, (the ecology check in well forming outcomes, see page 89) nothing will be taken away only new choices become available. This can build your expectations about what is possible. This is the power of belief, which is also one of the factors in hypnosis and the placebo effect.

I once took some photographs in a bar of a group of people I had been working with during the day. The next day I passed around some contact sheets and one woman was angry at the inclusion of pictures of her because she didn't want people she didn't know seeing them at some time in the future.

So I handed her the contact sheets and invited her to find some scissors and cut out the small pictures of herself. Eventually she found some scissors and carefully cut around the other pictures in order to remove several pictures of herself. This took her some time to do one sheet of contacts as she had to carefully cut around all the other little pictures and when she had finished this on one of the sheets she handed all the sheets back to me saying she couldn't be bothered to cut out the pictures on the other pages.

Later on that day I noticed her standing in a group photo and she seemed very relaxed doing that. Somehow her issue about being photographed had disappeared. I had turned her problem into a tedious task and somehow it wasn't there anymore. She didn't want or couldn't be bothered to do that anymore.

These are examples of bringing conscious awareness or thinking, in a different way, to bear on "problems" which are often activities we do unconsciously, so improving our self awareness and thereby learning that you can begin to change less than useful behaviours and habits and become more aware and mindful of your own thinking processes.

Carl Jung said: *"In order to change something, first we have to accept it."*

As Richard Bandler says: "Who's running your brain?"

For some people who grew up in families where there was a lot of arguments and sometimes violence going on, they developed their abilities to "read" and understand non-verbal signals and tone of voice of their parents or other adults as a survival strategy. For them it was very important to be able to read the visual cues or know from hearing a particular tone of voice that danger was imminent and anyone can learn these skills. They had trained their awareness in a particular way.

Having good general awareness can affect our physiology and send out certain messages to the world. Some psychologists set up an interesting experiment in New York. They positioned a camera overlooking a busy city street and left it on record for an hour.

They then took the video and showed it in local prisons and asked prisoners who were convicted of street robbery to pick out those people in the film who they would select to rob. The prisoners pretty much picked the same people and for the same reasons. They chose those people who they could tell from their body language were switched off and not paying attention to their surroundings.

AVOIDING STREET ROBBERY & CURING BACK PAIN

A good topical example of lack of awareness or putting their awareness in the wrong place, are people walking around talking or texting on their mobiles, which are then easily snatched, by people on foot or on cycles and motorcycles. I have seen this happen three times in London, and apparently this is the most common street crime in the capital right now.

Also, apparently, walking along with your head down while texting is the cause of a lot of back pain. Any Physiotherapist or Pilates Consultant will tell you about the strain caused by having the neck extended in that manner over a period of time.

When someone is walking in the street and using their mobile phones either for conversations or for texting it means that a large proportion of the person's conscious awareness is on the inside and not on the street. Their conscious attention is taken up by the phone conversation or texting and they are less aware of what's going on around them. This is also the reason that using a mobile while driving has been made illegal, in the UK at least.

The convicted robbers in the New York research project said that they were able to read people's body language such as having their head down, looking distracted and with invitations like an open bag or the shoulder strap over only one shoulder so that it is easy to snatch, in fact anything that sent out the signal "Easy Target".

A street robber is an opportunist and is generally skilled at reading signals and the last thing they want is a struggle or fight with someone. They want to get in and out fast and with the least amount of trouble. Drug addicts may be more desperate and take more chances and I have seen that happen where they get into a struggle while cutting through the strap on a person's bag.

There is another story of a British tourist who was visiting New York in the 1970s and had been warned about people getting mugged on the street and to be careful. One night he took a Taxi to meet some friends at a party in a less than OK neighbourhood. His friend left the party early and he eventually left at 2 or 3 in the morning and realised he was lost on a deserted street in a strange area of the city.

He walked along the sidewalk hoping to find a Taxi and soon spotted a man walking towards him. He crossed the street and the man in the distance crossed so they were now on the same sidewalk again, heading towards each other.

The tourist was by now so hyped up by this that he was convinced that the stranger was about to mug him. As they met he went to pass the man and they both stepped in the same direction and bumped into each other. He frantically struggled to pass the man and hurried on his way. He checked his pockets and couldn't find his wallet. He was so enraged he ran back down the street and jumped on the man's back shouting angrily.

"Give me the wallet, give me the wallet."

The man handed over his wallet and the tourist rushed off and finally made it back to his hotel room and there on the bedside table was his wallet and he realised he had just mugged the man in the street.

According to Judith Delozier there is always a kernel of truth in the big paranoia and it's a fine line between Saturday night and Sunday morning. We have to keep a balance between paranoia and recklessness and a lot of keeping ourselves safe is about having a good awareness, being mindful of our surroundings and using the resource of common sense.

An Aikido student once asked me for advice about something that had happened to a friend of his. He had left a Pub late one night and took a shortcut home through a dark alleyway. Before he got to the end he was confronted and attacked by three men who did some nasty things to him with a baseball bat and then took all his valuables.

He asked me what I thought this friend of his could do in those circumstances. I replied by asking what he was doing walking down a dark alley with no escape route, on his own late at night having probably drunk too much alcohol.

A lot of keeping ourselves safe is to use our much-underrated skill of common sense and in this particular case, take the longer and safer way home.

You don't need to be an expert martial artist to stay safe but you do need some of the skills they learn in order for you to be expert enough, such as awareness and common sense.

Peripheral Vision

"In the Art of Peace, we aim to see everything at once, taking in the entire field of vision in a single glance." – The Art of Peace, O Sensei.

Here's a simple exercise. Stand up and straighten your arms so your hands are directly in front of you at eye level. Keeping your eyes to your front and having and keeping soft focus of the eyes, slowly move your arms sideways and notice the point where you lose sight of your hands. For me it is about 90 degrees each way from the center and at the point where my hands are beginning to move behind me.

You have the ability to look to the front and at the same time see to the sides and you can take in large amounts of visual information all the time and consciously you are only aware of a very small amount of that information. However the rest is not lost or wasted but rather is taken in, processed and stored by the unconscious and often emerges in the form of a feeling which is a signal to be aware and pay attention.

When NLP co-founder, John Grinder, first came back to the UK to deliver some training in the early 90s, he told the following story.

One of his interests and passions was birds of prey. One day he was piloting a small plane above the California coastline. Suddenly he was confronted by a large bird of prey with its wings spread right in front of his cockpit window and his instantaneous reaction was to yank the joystick back to climb above the bird.

As he did this and looked down he saw an airliner flying inches beneath him in the opposite direction and he realised it hadn't been a bird of prey at all but his unconscious mind had produced that image knowing it would get the fastest reaction from him.

CHAPTER 6 – BECOME THE ENEMY

"Never judge a person until you have walked a mile in their moccasins." – Native American saying

PERCEPTUAL POSITIONS, A TRIPLE DESCRIPTION

Part of Musashi's teaching in "The Book of Five Rings" is "To become the enemy", think as if one were the enemy. He says:

"Even the thief who blockades himself in a house (when caught in the act) is considered by his opponents to be most formidable. But if you put yourself in his position, you can see that he feels helpless, that everyone in the world is against him. He who has blockaded himself is like a pheasant, while he who is waiting outside is like a hawk."

Some work was recently done with young criminals who were incarcerated in prison, some for life, after having committed violent crimes. Surviving victims and their family members agreed to participate in a project and were brought into the prison and talked to the perpetrators and told them their stories of how their lives had been totally devastated by the criminal act. They explained in detail the effects of the criminals' actions as they attacked and damaged their victims and the aftermath of that attack, both physical and psychological on both the victims and their families and friends.

What was really interesting and somewhat worrying was that none of these mostly, but not exclusively, young male criminals had any awareness of the impact and effects on their victims. They never went there in their thinking even as they were kicking their victim in the head and certainly never considered the consequences for themselves, their victims or the victims' families.

A friend who is a psychotherapist and Shodan Yudansha told me about a client he worked with many years ago who was a burglar. He said that one of the worse things to find in a house that he was robbing was a cat because it instantly told him that a family lived there. He had been triggered into empathy, his ruthlessness had gone and he started to feel guilty and usually left immediately.

What the criminals in prison were seeing and being told by the victims and their families shocked them and it had a profound influence on their future behaviour and reduced the levels of reoffending. I think that this is an on-going model being used in prisons right now.

In NLP the ability to see and feel and get an understanding of what is going on for others is called 2nd positioning someone, literally standing in his or her shoes and is also known as empathy. By doing this you are able to begin to pick up "intuitions" about what that person is seeing and feeling. The inability to do this is part of the cause of psychopathic behaviour.

Musashi said: *"Know the enemy. To become the enemy is to think as if one were the enemy."*

As a coach or anyone closely involved in teaching and caring for others, the skill is being able to experience the other person's feelings, see the world through their eyes and be aware of what is theirs and what is your own.

The ability to change your own perspective and see the bigger picture as well as being able to see things from another's point of view is an essential skill. In NLP this ability is known as taking different perceptual positions and there are in fact three positions we can take or be in.

The idea of multiple perceptual positions in NLP was originally inspired by Gregory Bateson's "triple description", which proposed that double or triple descriptions are better than one. By training in moving between perceptual positions you can get different information and develop a new choice of responses.

1st Position (Self) – this is where you are standing in your own shoes, fully associated in your feelings and looking at the world through your own eyes. This is a strong position to be in where you know what you want and are not necessarily concerned so much about what others want. You will be using "I" when referring to yourself.

However anyone who spends most of their time in this position may be regarded as arrogant, too direct, not caring or concerned with understanding others and what they may want.

2nd Position (Other) – known as empathy, this is where you are taking the viewpoint of another person or persons, seeing, disassociated from yourself, and associated in the other person and experiencing how the world is for them and this is an essential component of emotional intelligence, (see Daniel Goleman's book "Emotional Intelligence"). In this position you will refer to yourself as "you".

People who are in the caring professions such as nurses, doctors, therapists, coaches, teachers, police and paramedics etc. as well as parents, need to have the ability to take another's point of view.

Anyone who inhabits this perceptual position most of the time is in danger of becoming a "doormat" and constantly seeing others as more important and sometimes attempting to "rescue" them, not caring enough for themselves and seldom achieving their own outcomes.

My elderly mother has carers coming into her flat every day and you can definitely see this quality in them. They work very hard at looking after her and for not very much pay. They really do care.

3rd Position (Observer) – this is where you can step out and see yourself in a situation with others. This is an essential skill for gathering information in any relationship, teamwork, meeting, problem solving situation, negotiations, etc. You can become an observer like being the "fly on the wall" and can see yourself in the situation, check how well you are doing or otherwise and make any necessary adjustments.

Here you will be using he, she or they when speaking about yourself and others in the situation.

To be in this perceptual position is useful if you are a paramedic or policeman having to deliver bad news to someone or a surgeon who has to cut flesh. You wouldn't want to be in 2nd position and experiencing any feelings of pain or shock so it is a useful skill to be able to choose to be in a 3rd position and be disconnected to those feelings.

To inhabit this position continually means a person can come across as detached and not connected to their feelings which can cause problems in relationships.

Wisdom is being able to switch between these three different perceptual positions at will.

We can also use double and triple place disassociation to deal with bad memories, traumas that cause PTSD and Phobias.

CHARACTERLOGICAL ADJECTIVES – A PERCEPTUAL POSITION EXERCISE

The ability to step into someone else's shoes, see and feel the world as they do can be a useful tool to get new information, literally a different perspective, on a difficulty in any relationship.

Quite often I have heard people say something like: "if only he or she would change, everything would be alright."

They are not accepting that they are also in the communication loop and are putting all of the cause onto the other person.

Remember you cannot not communicate and therefore you cannot not have an influence.

- Imagine you are sitting in a theatre and there is a spotlight shining on the stage. A figure steps into the spotlight and you realise it is the person you are having difficulty with.

- What is a word that describes their behaviour in this situation?

  E. G. Angry, aggressive or attacking

- A second spotlight shines on the stage, take a deep breath and see yourself standing under that light. You are in the difficult situation with this other person and you, as the observer in the theatre, are now in third position, seeing yourself and the other person.

- What is a word that describes your behaviour in this situation?

  E. G. Defensive, withdrawn or retreating

- So both people are involved and the words describe both sides of the communication loop. Going to third position by sitting in the theatre and observing yourself with the other person enables you to see and understand your own part in this interaction as well as the other person and be able to get the information needed to change the dynamics in the relationship.

- What is needed here to change the situation, what resource could you bring to the relationship? It could be something like changing tone of voice or being more empathetic (2nd Position) with the other person.

Often we are colluding with the other person's behaviour. By being defensive or withdrawn we enable the other person to be angry or aggressive. Some people may have an attitude of:

"Why should I change what I'm doing, they should make an effort and change what they are doing."

Remember the conditions for a well-formed outcome, one of which, states that a well-formed goal cannot be dependant on what someone else does because they might not do it. So if you want to change the current impasse change your own behaviour and they will respond to that and, as in the TOTE model, make adjustments until you get the desired result.

You can also find this in relationships where one person is supporting the other who may have an addiction and despite destructive behaviours they continue to support or rescue them. Nothing will change until that "rescuing" behaviour changes in some way.

Treat them as if they are OK rather than being a victim in an "I'm OK, you're not OK" relationship. Better to be in an "I'm OK, you're OK" relationship that is the same as Win/Win, the desired result in any negotiation.

This is not about abandoning people only about introducing more choices, such as pacing and leading them to consider doing other things, such as setting goals and building positive images of their future and seeing themselves having already changed their behaviour in a useful way. This may not be the whole answer on its own but it is a start in a more useful direction and will certainly lead that person to better choices.

We can also think about this in Aikido or a "real" situation. If you are the defender it implies there is an attacker and one way to change this dynamic is to take action rather than staying as a defender.

Your action can be to "be present" so the other(s) can see that in your physiology and have to reconsider their proposed action, or move in first so the person can't attack properly or you can move away before anything happens so once again the dynamic is changed.

There is an Aikido principle called "Irimi" and its meaning is that you would enter, off the center line, towards an attack so you are repositioned next to and slightly behind the attacker and looking the same way as them. To accomplish this you need to blend with the attacker (Awase) and enter towards and past them, at the same time as the attack happens or initiate the attack yourself.

Aikido is full of paradox and irimi is one of them. For most people their immediate reaction to an attack is to withdraw and the idea of stepping towards an attack is alien. When this move is done well their attack moves past you into the "hole" you have created, they are momentarily off balance and you are both facing the same way, so you are matching and any problem is now out there in front of both of you. Irimi will also enable you to deal with more than one person as you can move out of the circle of attackers.

In a communication situation this would be a good time to stand next to the other person and point to the problem in front of you both and go to "we" in your language. This is a very useful strategy in a business situation and you can write the issue on a whiteboard or flip chart, then stand side by side and gesture towards the problem out there, in front of both of you. Now you are both working together to deal with the problem, you have the same outcome, a mutual goal.

You can also do this with language like the old man in the story at the beginning. He entered (irimi) with his voice, not in an aggressive way, loud but not louder than the drunk man, it matched his energy, his tone of voice made clear he was non judgemental and expressed a curiosity in what the man had been drinking and they had something they could talk about.

He had lead the man out of his problem state by switching to a very different subject, i.e. the persimmon tree, a different place that was able to elicit a very different state to anger like sadness that is quieter. One intervention by the old man had an instant and effective change in the situation.

This is a linguistic strategy used in NLP and Hypnosis and is called a "Pattern Interrupt". It gets the person's attention and sort of stops them in their tracks but in a non-threatening way.

When O Sensei was asked what he would do if someone attacked him he replied:

"Why would anyone attack me when I am in harmony with the universe?"

– **Chunking**

"How do you eat an elephant?"

Remember the book I referred to earlier, "The Structure of Magic", the first NLP book, all about language, published back in 1975. When I first experienced this material on a NLP Practitioner course it mostly went right over my head. I just didn't get it. I realised if I wanted to be a good NLP coach I needed to read and understand this material.

As you can imagine it is quite a technical book and I wasn't at all familiar with the idea of thought at the deep structure and its transformation by deletion, distortion and generalisation on its way to the surface structure. I hope you are still with me?

So I had to have a way of getting through this book and understanding the material and I knew if I sat down at home and attempted to read it I would quickly get distracted and/or fall asleep.

At that time I was working part time in a College in Acton in West London and I had to travel by underground there and back every working day and that took 40 minutes each way. I knew I could concentrate on the book for that amount of time and managed to read the whole book 3 times in a year, by which time I had pretty much got it.

This is an example of chunking and is very useful in any context and particularly when taking in new information and learning. The process of learning Aikido is an example of chunking, learning techniques in part and in whole over and over until it is in the muscle and then continuing to study and hone the same basics and principles underlying the techniques.

American psychologist, George Miller, carried out some research in the 1950s and published a paper entitled: "The Magic Number Seven, Plus or Minus 2.

He discovered that human beings are only able to keep track of seven plus or minus two pieces of information in working memory consciously, which means in present moment awareness.

Depending on the context and our stress levels the seven chunks will increase to nine or decrease to five or less chunks of information. This means that there are thousands of pieces of information that are going to the unconscious part of the brain which is like the hard drive of a computer that can store and process limitless amounts of data and run programs automatically.

Recent research has demonstrated that not only is this meaning based on a misinterpretation of Miller's paper, but that the correct number is probably as low as three bits of information and according to Daniel Goleman in his book "Focus" the use of laptops, tablets and mobile phones has reduced our ability to focus down to one thing at a time.

An example of "overload" was one time I was teaching an aikidoka a series of techniques that he had to perform for a grading. When we got to about number eleven he knelt on the mat and said he could no longer remember anything. He looked flushed and was in a state of information overload, not conducive to high performance.

What I did then was to "chunk" the information into groups. So many techniques from this attack and so many from a different attack meant he had to remember five groups instead of 15 or more techniques. Thinking about each group enabled him to remember the techniques within the groups.

Another example of chunking and our ability to remember, or not, are telephone numbers. As more and more numbers are used new codes have been added before the number itself and we are over the edge of our ability to remember whole numbers, so we tend to chunk our phone numbers into sections or blocks which can then be recalled.

It is useful to remember this principle in many different contexts such as when we are making things like lists, agendas, documents, emails, in fact any communication. If you want to get peoples attention in marketing material keep it to a few main points so that they are not overloaded.

COMMUNICATING WITH YOUR UNCONSCIOUS MIND

There are many examples of the unconscious working away on your behalf such as running your heart at the correct rate or near enough and you don't generally have to think consciously about all the tiny muscles that need to operate when you smile or the process of breathing. You can think of them consciously if you want but you don't need to and you can rely on them working excellently in the background.

Your habits are examples of activities, both physical and mental, that have been wired in by many repetitions until you don't have to think about what you are doing. This includes habits that are not useful and may hold you back and keep you in the same place, possibly an example of serving some sort of purpose for you, i.e. the positive intention to and for you of that "limitation".

Here is an example of something you have learnt so well you can just leave it to your unconscious.

Cross your arms across your chest the way you usually do, for example left arm over right arm. Its easy for you isn't it? You don't have to consciously think about what you are doing with your arms, you can just do it.

Now try this:

Cross your arms across your chest again but this time do it the opposite way to what you usually do.

Not so easy or smooth, is it? Now you have to consciously think about which arm goes where and it probably feels a bit uncomfortable and probably takes longer to your usual way.

This is an example of knowing something at the level of unconscious competence, the ability to cross your arms with ease, changing that sequence and suddenly it feels a bit awkward and takes you back to conscious incompetence.

Continue to practice the new way and after you have repeated this new way enough times you get to conscious competence and then unconscious competence again. Now you no longer have to think about what you are doing and you can comfortably leave the operation to your unconscious. It is, once more, a well-honed habit and you have learnt a new way of doing it, more choice.

Ever had the experience of driving somewhere and when you reached your destination you realised you couldn't remember driving there? So who was driving? You were of course but you weren't consciously thinking about the operation of driving because all the skills were already learnt and are wired in after many repetitions.

The unconscious is where your resources are stored and the more you can learn to communicate with your unconscious the more you can open a portal (a doorway, gate, or other entrance) and have more access to these resources.

You will have different ways now to be able to do this, a sort of tool kit to enable you to be more mindful of your thinking process and make the most of the brain's ability.

It is said we are only using 8 - 10% of the potential of the brain.

*"The **10 percent** of the brain myth is a widely perpetuated urban legend that most or all humans only use **10 percent** (or some other small percentage) of their brains and this statement has been misattributed to many people, including Albert Einstein)."* – Wikipedia

Michelangelo, in answer to the question about how he made his beautiful sculptures said:

"Every block of stone has a statue inside it and it is the task of the sculptor to discover it. Carving is easy, you just go down to the skin and stop."

Carl Jung said: *"The message is in the symptom"* It is a signal or communication from the unconscious.

Learning to communicate with our own unconscious is like building rapport with our selves, or as Psychotherapist, Stephen Gilligan calls it "Self Relations". For example, paying attention and responding to symptoms as messages from our own unconscious and understanding their positive intention can initiate healing.

I once worked with a client, a woman who had the unusual symptom of not being able to keep her eyes open. She had to hold her eyelid up with her finger. She had already been operated on and a sling arrangement had been inserted into her eyebrow to keep her eyelid open.

She said this had been very painful, hadn't worked very well and she was due in the hospital for another operation later that week and was desperate to avoid that. She was brought to see me and I worked with her using NLP techniques and hypnosis and managed to get a positive result.

The positive intention of that behaviour or symptom was to protect her. There was literally too much for her to look at as her husband had recently died and she was left to deal with all of his business interests. She had never had to do anything like that and couldn't even write a cheque and her unconscious had literally "pulled down the shutters" to protect her.

I advised her to postpone the surgery as long as her eyelids worked correctly. Unfortunately when she telephoned the hospital and explained to the doctor what she had done with me and no longer wanted the surgery he told her it wouldn't last and persuaded her to book in for the surgery. She did this and I found out later that it had not worked.

This was a lesson for me. I should have included some "inoculation" for her so that she would have been able to resist the Doctor's advice, at least long enough to give our work a chance to succeed.

Robert Dilts has written a series of books called "Strategies of Genius" in which he presented his results of modelling people regarded as Genius. He did this from their writings and in some cases, recordings of them and films as well. One of the things he discovered was that they all had ways of accessing and utilising their unconscious resources.

Albert Einstein would work on a problem consciously until he recognised he could go no further and at that point he would let go of the problem and hand it over to his unconscious and go sailing in his dinghy in New York harbour.

In the July-August 2013 issue of Harvard Business Review there is an interesting article by Adam Waytz and Malia Mason entitled "Your Brain at Work, what a new approach to neuroscience can teach us about management."

Their recent discovery in neuroscience is that the brain is never really at rest and during waking periods when your brain is not focused on any particular thought and is wandering or zoned out, a brain region fires up which is called the "default" network. This discovery leads Waytz and Mason to believe that having unfocused free time is an important factor in breakthrough innovations.

Some organisations such as Google, Twitter and Maddock Douglas (marketing firm) offer staff days off to free associate in order to develop new ideas and achieve the "Eureka" moment. However detachment at work is difficult because employees' time is not exactly free and there is the expectation to come up with something and that means that their default networks don't detach from external stimuli and are still rooted in immediate reality.

They conclude we should experiment with total detachment, because it's a better way to generate breakthrough ideas. Rather than working hard, work smart which is not working at all, at least until new ideas have emerged.

Daydream to Success

In order to generate more ideas and be more creative, it is better to engage in some sort of "mindless" activity that enables the mind to wander rather than just doing nothing. NLP developed some processes called "Personal Editing Formats" during its early days that did exactly that. They were designed to get your conscious mind to concentrate on something completely different to your problem so allowing the unconscious mind to present you with ideas, questions and information.

In Aikido we are moving and I have heard Aikido described as "moving meditation." In coaching we are sitting although in NLP coaching a lot of the work is experiential, i.e. we physically move. The process of getting centered requires you to stand and experience your present stability or lack of and then the adjustments you make to be even more centered.

As a coach to sit or stand next to my client is very much like aligning myself and blending as in Aikido.

Being present/centered in Aikido and coaching is essential otherwise nothing works very well, if at all.

Think of a problem, let go of it and then spend maybe 10-15 minutes doing the process that could be something as simple as walking and then come back to the problem.

Often it has changed and no longer looks or feels like a problem. It is the total concentration on something detached from the problem that enables a solution to emerge.

"Solvitur ambulando – it is solved by walking." – Latin proverb.

Neuroscientists are now able to monitor activity in the brain via an EEG cap making multiple connections to the skull. This enables us to understand why "mind wandering" can be so effective in generating new ideas and solutions.

When people have what we call an insight, alpha waves occur in the rear of the right brain hemisphere that has the effect of shutting down the visual cortex, cutting off distractions and this is immediately followed by gamma wave activity in the right side of the right brain hemisphere as the insight occurs.

The brain sort of blinks and allows any insight to bubble up to the surface.

During Einstein's sailing breaks new ideas would "bubble up" from his unconscious, often in the form of questions. For example: "What would it be like if I was sitting on the end of a beam of light and travelling through space? If I held a mirror in front of me would I see my own reflection?"

In order for Einstein to answer these questions he had to go to a different perceptual position and get a different perspective from which he was able to get other information that had not, until then, been available to him.

He said: *"You cannot solve a problem at the same level of thinking that created the problem."* Often people are trying to solve their problems when they are in a "problem state" so they are bringing that sort of thinking to the problem solving process.

Problem thinking and the inner state associated with it is not the best kind of thinking to bring to problem solving, creativity or high performance, so having ways to be able to work "outside the box" and access resourceful states is essential for anyone who aspires to operate in an excellent way. Effective learning and problem solving is state dependent and being able to manage your own state is a prerequisite for effective leadership and excellence in any context.

Any repetitive physical action can help because your mind can wander freely allowing new ideas to emerge from the unconscious mind. In the martial arts we are constantly practising moves and techniques over and over and we also do what are called "katas" which are sequences of moves repeated many times, constantly honing them.

These sorts of physical activities partially shut down frontal lobe activity allowing an increased flow of creativity. Rex Jung, an Assistant Professor of Neurosurgery at the University of New Mexico in Albuquerque and a distinguished Senior Advisor to the Positive Neuroscience Project, based at the University of Pennsylvania, has shown that the frontal lobes act as an inhibitor, a gatekeeper and this temporary shut down removes our inhibitions.

This scientific work is still going on and we already know what to do in order to access these problem solving and creative states. We have a set of tools to enable us to do that.

Charles Darwin lived in a house in Kent, South East England and the garden had a very large garden. He had a pathway built around the perimeter of the garden and piles of stones were placed at intervals around the path. Whenever he had a problem he was stuck with, he would go for a walk around the garden on his "thinking path" and at some point a solution would emerge.

Eventually he was able to say:

"I'm going for a walk. I think this is a two pile of stones problem".

When Regan and Gorbachev were negotiating the de-escalation of nuclear weapons at Camp David and they were unable to make an agreement, they left their large teams of negotiators inside the building while they went for a walk on their own in the surrounding woods. It was during this walk that they were able to decide to come to an agreement and then instructed their teams to take care of the details.

Quite often when I am designing a workshop and get stuck I go and do a bit of ironing or spend a few minutes juggling and almost immediately ideas present themselves and I have to write them down at once, before I forget them, making sure I don't leave the hot iron on the shirt or gi (training suit).

What ways do you have of "turning off or zoning out?" Maybe you go fishing or walking, perhaps you like gardening, dancing or drawing and painting. Times where you can let go of any problems and allow ideas to present themselves. Before you start the process take a minute to think about the problem or maybe it's a goal or situation you want to improve and then let go of it completely and start your activity. When you have done about 10 minutes or more take another think about the issue. How is it now?

Maybe it doesn't feel like a problem any more and be alert for any ideas or questions that bubble up (like Einstein in his boat). What you have done is hand the issue over to your own unconscious mind so allow it to do what it is good at which is generating ideas and solutions. Recycle through this process if necessary and for even more ideas.

One of the NLP Personal Editing processes I am particularly fond of is called "The Alphabet Chart" and I have placed a copy of it in the Appendices, page 282.

At first glance it may look and seem a bit absurd but it is surprisingly effective. I used to be a bit nervous of using this process when training groups, especially business people, but found that they really enjoyed doing it and were impressed with the results they got.

The process involves editing an experience by splitting channels of attention.

- Choose a recurring situation where you want to have more choices for responding.

- Go through the chart as follows:

    Say out loud each letter. You can see L, R or T under each of the letters and they mean: Left, Right or Together. As you say the alphabet letter raise your left hand where you see the letter L, right hand for the letter R and both hands together for the letter T.

    When you get to the end reverse the process until you get back to the beginning. You can also then go up and down the columns.

- When you have finished, think about the situation again and notice what changes you experience in how you perceive or respond to that situation.

How do you feel different about it now? Perhaps you see or hear information that wasn't previously available to you and which makes a difference in how you respond. You might realise that you had been focussed on a certain part of the situation and are now able to see a wider perspective after doing this exercise.

CHAPTER 7 –
RELATIONSHIP & NON-CONFLICT

"Martial Arts begin and end with courtesy"

Building rapport with others or self is a key skill in NLP and Aikido. Rapport does not mean having to like someone or take on their beliefs but is rather a way of building a field of trust with the other person so that they feel comfortable, you make a connection and your communication can then take place easily.

You may have had the experience of being with someone you feel very comfortable and relaxed with and you are able to talk to them easily and with a sense of comfort and the opposite may be the case with some other person.

Rapport is created or built by matching the other person in any way possible. Mostly this is done with our physiology. We can match body positions, the tone, volume and speed of voice, breathing, language (use their words) as well as beliefs and values and even clothes. Think about uniforms and clothes that are acceptable for work such as some sort of overalls if you are doing something mechanical or if you are going to an interview for a job in a Bank, it's probably a good idea to wear a suit and match their dress culture.

"Fashion is the art of being the same with a difference". I said that and for some people it will be about being different with a bit of sameness.

We belong to clubs and societies with people who have similar interests and values. The more you can match others the more you can build rapport. We cannot not communicate and therefore we cannot not influence. Our very presence will have an effect even if we are not talking.

Some of my friends and colleagues have told me about times when they are finding it difficult to communicate with someone like their parents and always get into disagreements with particular people and end up bickering and find themselves in arguments.

These verbal conflicts usually take place face to face and they have been surprised at how they can listen and have reasonable conversations about their differences when they are travelling in a car and the person is sitting next to them.

In this situation they are in physical rapport, sitting side by side and facing the same way. All the wind has gone out of both their sails and any problem or difficulty is out in front of them, a different perspective.

Try in vain to have an argument with someone when you are sitting or standing side by side. This is a useful tool to align yourself with the other person so you are both referring to any problem as being out there in front of both of you, use "we" when talking about the issue and you are not only being in rapport but have switched perceptual positions in relation to the problem.

This is the same as "irimi" in Aikido as previously mentioned. From a face-to-face position you enter to their rear, turn by changing hanmi and you are then facing the same way as the "attacker" whose energy and momentum has taken them forward and off balance.

"To extend or lead in Aikido is to continue moving in the direction of the attack. This movement unbalances the attacker, who can then be redirected. Aikido allows the "completion of everyone's mission." – O Sensei

In Aikido the key to non-conflict is also through matching, blending and connecting and being in time with the other person's movement and momentum to take their balance by extending them off their center and then leading them in whatever way you want. Therefore there is no clash of power, strength, conflict or struggle and if there is then it is not Aikido.

If they raise their hand to attack you, then the awase is to match that upward movement and move in on them as they are raising their hand, so taking their balance before they can deliver a strike or moving to their rear as in irimi where you have a choice of a technique or just walking away.

Any attack that comes from someone in front of you can be dealt with by blending, moving in and turning so you are facing the same way as the attacker and are standing by their side or to their rear. The energy and momentum from their strike or attempted grab takes them forward and off balance like when you push on a door as it's opened from the other side and you stumble into the space. It is amazing how much of your energy is contained in that movement to open the door. The resistance to that energy has gone and there is no longer any conflict! In a real situation you would then have a choice to do something further to them or simply walk or run away.

When O Sensei was challenged he would move so that he was beside them or to their rear and they were never able to touch him and they often, as a result of this experience, would then become his student.

We know that by matching people we not only build rapport but also we begin to get into their skin and get intuitions about what they are feeling and importantly their intention so we are connected to them. A lot of Aikido training is about Awase, constantly blending, not struggling and this requires a lot of conscious concentration, being present inside the rhythm of their movement. Physical mindfulness, when the body knows what to do and responds immediately, meaning fractions of a second, no time taken to think first, just a physical response.

I was sitting in my car waiting, as if parked, for a car coming the other way and as that car passed by and I began to move forward, an interesting thing happened. Just as the car began to move, the rear passenger door on the driver side opened, I instantly turned around and a figure almost began to step in and I heard a soft exclamation. At the same time I realised what had happened.

The door slammed shut at the same I stopped the car. I saw a blue car coming up behind and saw a woman stepping in. I was in a blue car and the woman had seen it begin to move and instantly opened the door to my car and I then saw her car was also blue. She had mistaken my car for hers and quickly tried to get in and then realising it was the wrong car and quickly getting back out.

I thought about this during the next week and particularly that moment when I heard and felt the passenger door open. There was something about how the door was "snapped" open, an urgency that I had felt and helped me make that instantaneous response.

It was a woman and she had mistaken my car for her family car that her husband was driving and when she saw the first bit of movement of the car she had snatched the door open, panicking thinking she was missing her ride and immediately realising it was the wrong car and slamming the door. All of this happened probably in less than a second and my thinking that week was that there had not been any thought, just my physical response but actually all of that thinking and making meanings had happened.

I recently saw a concert of Boy-band, "Take That" on TV. They used to have 5 members and are now down to 3 and to do this "come-back" concert with only 3 members was a concern and challenge for them. They had put together a large troupe of dancers, an excellent band and a colourful and complicated stage production. It was a bit like Pop's version of Pink Floyd and it was very slick.

They had been performing together for 20 years and obviously knew each other very well. They rehearsed the show over and over and on the night they were stunningly perfect. Completely in sync and it reminded me of when I am training with someone and we are doing something like the Kimusubi awase series with swords. The moment you are not present with your partner you will be slightly behind. It's a very powerful feeling when you know you are together and could lead if necessary.

The "Take That" audience have followed the group and know every song and sing every word with the band, a huge choir and the feeling of rapport that is generated is on a powerfully huge scale and is an example of group consciousness. They become one entity.

I loved the close up shots of the audience members singing along with the band. They knew every word and put so much energy into it with joy and enthusiasm.

I am not particularly a fan of "Take That" but I do appreciate excellence when I see it.

When we are training and learning a technique and find ourselves struggling and resorting to using force and muscle power, then we know we are doing it wrong and need to look for the correct angle and path of no resistance. This is the learning process, a dynamic feedback system and I think one of the biggest learnings is to understand this, leave the ego behind and then change what you are doing.

Where and when we hit a "bump", it's like the NLP Presupposition says: "There's no such thing as failure only feedback." We take stock; look for an adjustment until we find that path. Aikido is full of paradox. Opposite and equal and often unequal power in the other person's favour is not going to work if we continue to confront their strength, so we can adjust our position and let their energy go in the direction they are pushing or pulling.

Power comes from pushing out of the ground in a rising spiral and if you push directly into someone you will be stopped but change the angle and push up and they can't stop you and what goes up must come down so having shifted their balance we can then bring them down or rather we put them in a position where they can't avoid falling.

There is a NLP model called T.O.T.E. This stands for Test, Operate, Test and Exit. This model is a description of the fundamental feedback loop, which is the basis for all mental process and behaviour.

It is a way of monitoring your mental processes. Are you achieving what you want, the test, if so exit and move on, if not, do something else, another operation, then check, test again, until you are getting what you want and then exit?

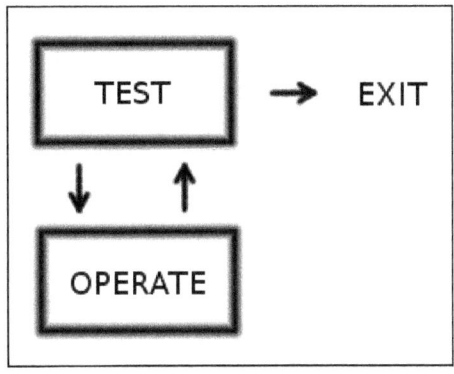

The Tote Model

Remember our "Success Strategy" – Outcome, Awareness and Flexibility so we need to have flexibility around our fixed goals. When we are not getting what we want, that is feedback to change what we are doing.

The process of blending in Aikido is called "Awase" and is one of the basic principles and skills of both NLP and Aikido. Remember, when asked what he would do if someone attacked him, O Sensei replied:

"Why would someone attack me when I am in harmony with the Universe?"

Sometimes when life gets busy and the pressure is on or something surprises us, we are disturbed and lose our mental balance or center. We have allowed ourselves to be extended away from our center, mentally, and this will be demonstrated in our physiology and our performance.

"Before you think about something, think about how you want to think about It." – Gregory Bateson

You have probably heard this already. It is not the difficulties in life that are important; it is how we cope with the difficulties that is important and the place to start is with your own state.

Entrepreneur James Clear says:

"Top performers still find a way to show up, to work through the boredom, and to embrace the daily practice that is required to achieve their goals."

According to him, it's this ability to do the work when it's not easy that separates the top performers from everyone else and it's the difference between professionals and amateurs. Entrepreneur Tai Lopez calls this the daily grind. You have to keep going and work through it.

An Aikido Sensei talked about the importance of remaining cool and calm when in a stressful situation, be it verbal, physical or both and one way to do this is contained in how you present yourself. This is what the Samurai did. They trained and trained to build their skills that also built their confidence and their goal was always to be calm.

AIKIDO – THE WAY OF THE SWORD WITH NO SWORD

Correct Posture is Power

If you set yourself obviously tense and looking ready for physical action or your hands are raised, this can leave openings and encourage conflict. Best to remain physically and mentally cool and calm and one way to do this is to assume the position of "hanmi".

Hanmi means "half body". This is the idea that the sides of the body work as a unit (for example: right hand and right foot forward).

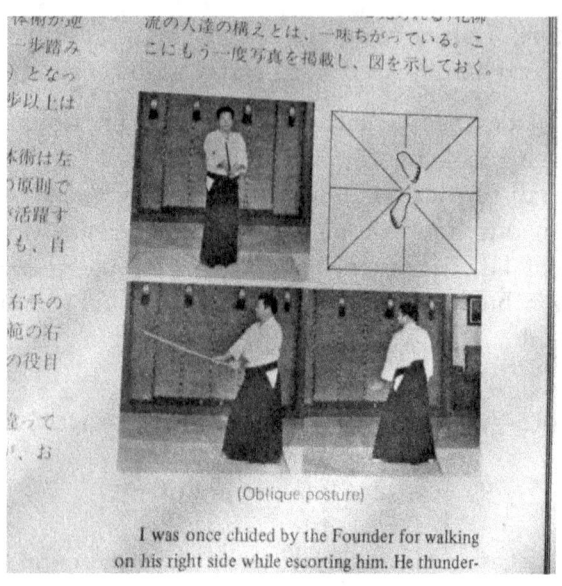

(Oblique posture)

I was once chided by the Founder for walking on his right side while escorting him. He thunder-

Hanmi comes from the use of the sword and the spear and is the basis of all Aikido. One of the purposes of weapons training in Aikido is to teach the body certain positions and ways to move so we are always centred and moving as if we are holding a sword.

One foot is placed in front of the other. The heel of the front foot lines up with the base of the big toe of the rear foot which is turned outwards, both feet then forming a triangle and the shoulder and hip are turned slightly forward so all the vital organs and vulnerable points are protected and no openings are given, unless it is bait. This position also facilitates the ability to spontaneously respond and move in any direction.

This was described to me by a Sensei as "silent body language". An inner stillness so that you can respond immediately or anticipate the other person's movement and there is no twitching of the hands first, no redundant body language. The body or center moves before the hands and legs.

When standing waiting to receive an "attack" you should see everything, watch the other person's body with soft focus of your eyes, not watching their hands or weapon if they are carrying one. This is where you will see their first movement, in the body, in the breathing. One of the most powerful ways to build rapport and connect in NLP and Hypnosis is to match the breathing of the other person.

So receiving an attack is not a passive action. We are present and presenting ourselves in a way that determines their attack and we can also learn their intention as previously mentioned by matching and joining them and as Musashi said: *"Become the enemy"*.

Some years ago I helped a colleague who was training some young high flyers for an international organisation. When I arrived I was introduced to the Director who had designed the course and was responsible for selecting the content and the Trainers.

Later I was sitting at the side of the training room with about 20 minutes of the afternoon's programme to go when the door opened and the Director walked in. As the group were still working he came and sat next to me and to fill the time as we couldn't talk I decided to micro match him in all the ways I could, particularly his breathing. I did this very carefully so he couldn't consciously notice what I was doing. When matching is done carelessly and in a gross way, much like kids playing a mimicry game, then it tends to lose rapport.

When the course finished I turned and said something like: "So you're the man who designed this programme for high flyers." It wasn't a question. He started talking and he told me some interesting facts about what his future plans were, his current budgets and his criteria for selecting Trainers.

I was able to pass on this information to my colleague, which consequently could have been useful, if he was interested in getting more work from the organisation. It hadn't been my intention or goal to get that information but it is an example of what can happen when strong rapport is built.

THE PRINCIPLE OF MATCHING

"When people do as they please, they usually imitate each other."

– Eric Hoffer

合 – ai – joining, unifying, combining, fit

In Aikido we have the idea of connecting with the other person so there is no conflict. Kimusubi is the act or process of matching one's partner's movement and intention at its inception, and maintaining a connection throughout the application of an aikido technique. Kimusubi is like entwined energy or ki and requires a mind that is clear, flexible, and attentive.

In paired sword work the decisive stroke or cut is where, with the use of hanmi, the other's "centre line" has been taken leaving them exposed. This requires that connection, kimusubi, and failure to do this will result in "ai uchi" or mutual kill. The difference is seemingly small but the consequences are huge.

As a result of the initial modeling (studies) of excellent performers made by Richard Bandler and John Grinder in the early seventies, the ways in which human beings communicate and build relationships has been taught on NLP Trainings and is one of the basics that we need to be aware of and utilise.

Now it's not essential to be in rapport all the time and there may be occasions when you want to break rapport. The most extreme way of doing this is to turn your back to the other person but you can do things like turn slightly away and break eye contact or mismatch physically in some other way. Most people can get the message from this and begin to end the contact.

This is something most politicians choose to ignore and they will continue to talk even when someone else is talking and maybe trying to get them to stop. It's a pointless exercise because someone listening can't hear what he or she are saying but they are so programmed to keep talking and to be seen and heard to be putting out the party "line of the day", they ignore the obvious non-verbal feedback. Surely they must know this and therefore I presume they trade getting their message across for the status of being last man or woman talking and their goal becomes just to stop others from talking.

They are not noticing the responses they are getting so no wonder we are all so frustrated with them and when you think about what they are doing, it is really very clumsy and ineffective other than preventing proper examination of what they are saying.

I recommend they do some research around cognitive bias and learn how they are being run by their own biases and beliefs despite information and evidence to the contrary.

Here's a definition of cognitive bias:

"A **cognitive bias** refers to a systematic pattern of deviation from norm or rationality in judgment, whereby inferences about other people and situations may be drawn in an illogical fashion. Individuals create their own "subjective social reality" from their perception of the input".

They are operating in a "Fixed Loop" as Matthew Sayid says in his book "Black Box Thinking" and this means they are ignoring and not accepting feedback. The most important learnings are contained in mistakes and errors. I'm sure I am making a generalisation here but most politicians on the public circuit operate like this. It's almost as if they are building a wall to keep out all that pesky information and maybe people, us, the electorate, eventually get fed up with that and are then motivated to elect someone else.

The important thing is to know how human beings can create "Rapport" or relationship between themselves and others by matching or mirroring the other person's physiology, voice, language, values and clothes. You probably won't find any rapport being used in disagreements; arguments or conflict situations and the introduction of "Rapport" can often be enough to begin to change those situations.

The difference that makes the difference with sales people is in their ability to build relationships with their customers or potential customers rather than going for a quick one-off sale.

The more we can be like others, stand in their shoes, look similar, have the same interests and do similar activities by joining clubs and associations, the more we are able to create a connection, feel comfortable with others and communicate clearly. Even though people do tend to like others who are like them this does not mean we have to like the others or agree with their beliefs and values, rather, by matching, you create a space where others feel safe and communication happens easily and this is how we build communities.

We can acknowledge someone's belief or value but we don't have to take it on as our own. People are entitled to their own beliefs and remember a belief is not the "truth" or "reality". It is simply a belief, a generalisation and filter on the world.

However people will fight and die over their beliefs. Take a look around the world. Most of the "wars" are being fought over beliefs about religion, ownership of territory and resources, having better systems of government, talking about being right and this is something you hear politicians such as Tony Blair and the present incumbent saying. "I am doing this because I believe it is right". One of the NLP responses to that would be:

"Right for whom?" It certainly wasn't right for all those thousands of civilians killed in Iraq.

Here is another way to address that by pacing:

"Yes that is your belief and I have another way to think about it."

Or

"Well that belief may be true in YOUR model of the world, but in my model of the world..."

All of the ways of building rapport we do naturally and mostly unconsciously, especially with family, friends and other people we know well. When people are in Rapport it is like a dance, in harmony with each other and it is mostly happening unconsciously. If, like me, you are someone who processes information a lot through the kinesthetic system then you will feel it when someone mismatches you and it can kill a conversation stone dead.

One of the most successful contemporary activities that people participate in is the collective experience of dance music with everybody doing the same thing, being in harmony is what makes it so successful, being In rapport creates an amazing feeling in the group.

Be mindful about your own feelings in response to how others speak to you. I went to the box office to pick up some cinema tickets that I had earlier booked and paid for online. I knew I was supposed to present a copy of the confirmation email but my printer had run out of ink and the person sitting in the box office said something like:

"What you haven't got the confirmation?" He spoke rather abruptly and when I walked away I noticed I felt a bit chastised. He told me I had to collect the tickets in the foyer of the cinema where a similar interaction occurred and I was told to pay in the cinema next time rather than book on line. Once again I noticed how I felt in response to being told this. They weren't exactly being rude but I could sense their struggle to restrain themselves. I know they were trying to get me to follow a designated procedure but basically they didn't help me feel welcome so not the greatest of customer care.

I think most people are not consciously aware of this but still experience the negative feeling, walk away and put up with how they are treated. There is always so much opportunity to practice being mindful and managing how we want to feel.

One of the things that we do when someone mismatches us is to make meanings about him or her such as that they are not listening to us; they are bored and not interested or even that they don't like us. So it can be very important for you to be aware of this and depending on what your outcome is, consciously check whether you are matching the other person.

If this communication is important to you make sure you match their physiology and play back some of their words to them. Like most things it requires practice and you will be surprised how good you can get at building rapport and begin to appreciate the effects and improved results you can create.

The founders of NLP modeled these principles from excellent communicators and they have been taught on NLP courses ever since. The principle of matching or mirroring is the basis of effective communication and a key to non-conflict.

You might have seen a movie, starring Kevin Costner, who befriends a wild wolf and engages in games with the wolf causing the Native Americans to name him "Dances With Wolves." Apparently it was not unusual for Native Americans to have friendly relationships with wild wolves and unlike the myths created about wolves by settlers, Indians maintained a close and respectful relationship with wolves.

They had found a way to live in harmony with them.

O Fred Donaldson Ph.D. taught geography, Black studies and Native American Studies at the University of

Washington and was engaged in a long-term study of wolves and having spent time studying and being with them gained the trust of a pack of seven wolves. His ability to do this was based on his study of their behaviors and the principles of blending learnt from his many years training as an Aikidoka.

His Aikido experience helped him participate in a wolf chase game that looks like a contest but is actually play. A wolf picks up a stick in its jaws and begins to run and the other wolves give chase. After a brief time the wolf drops the stick that was then picked up by another wolf and the chase continued.

Fred Donaldson noticed that the wolf in the lead runs at just less than maximum speed thereby inviting pursuit. The lead wolf not only doesn't try to get away but also glances back to check that she is being pursued. The pursuing wolves do not try to catch the wolf with the stick and if the lead wolf runs at full speed it then becomes a contest, or as its no longer a game, the pack doesn't chase anymore.

This reminds me of "ki no nagare" Aikido, that is practice on the move, where an attack is anticipated, blended with and a technique executed. If the practitioner's timing is out and they move late they will be grabbed or hit and if they move too far ahead of their partner then there is no need for their partner to follow and he or she would then be able to retreat or make a different attack. With good timing or awase the person is committed to the attack and their balance can be taken. They feel that they can get hold or strike the other person but good awase means they fall into the space you have created by matching, moving and leading them.

The same applies with NLP when we match and lead and if the other person does not follow we need to go back to matching and then, like the wolves, wait until they do follow.

Extraordinary scientific confirmation of this activity of matching came, almost by accident, serendipity I guess, when a group of Neuro Scientists was working in Parma University in Milan in the early 1990s. They were studying the brain in relation to motor movement and were using macaque monkeys to aid their research. The monkeys' brains were wired to computers via attachments stuck to the outside of their skulls and any activation of cells in a particular area of the brain under investigation would generate both visual and auditory signals from the computer.

One day the lab was empty and when one of the Neuro Scientists entered and reached to pick up some food from a table, one of the monkeys was sitting in its cage watching and suddenly static noise from a computer suddenly started and when he looked at the screen all sorts of things were happening with brain traces. Certain cells in the motor area of the hand and arm in the monkey's brain were being activated even though the monkey was not doing anything. On further investigation it was discovered that there are cells in the brain and our second brain, the enteric nervous system or gut, which are known as Mirror Neurons, and they are fired when another person is observed doing something. We are literally matching what others are doing in our brains.

Incidentally, the gut has a mind of its own, the "enteric nervous system". Just like the larger brain in the head, researchers say, this system sends and receives impulses, records experiences and responds to emotions. Its nerve cells are bathed and influenced by the same neurotransmitters, hence the expression: "gut reaction".

When the monkey reaches and picks something up cells are fired throughout the whole grasping action. The same thing will happen when the monkey sees another doing the same activity whether its a monkey or a human and it can also be the memory of action, a cognitive process.

Mirror neurons fired in a monkey when another monkey picked up something and it doesn't matter what the object is but size makes a difference. Different mirror neurons will fire when a small object such as a raison is picked up because it requires more precision with the fingers so different muscles are being used. Mirror Neurons provide a key mechanism for understanding the mental states and intentions of others by stimulating them in our own brain.

According to Marco Iacoboni in his book "Mirroring People":

"We achieve our very subtle understanding of other people thanks to certain collections of special cells in the brain called mirror neurons. These are the tiny miracles that get us through the day. They are at the heart of how we navigate through our lives. They bind us with each other, mentally and emotionally."

This explains why visualizing your-self doing something well is an effective learning tool as all the appropriate neurons are firing and creating or adding to the relevant neural pathways necessary to perform the activity.

THE BRAIN GYM AND THE STRUCTURE OF INFLUENCE

A study, by Dr. Blaslotto at the University of Chicago, was conducted where he put basketball players into three groups and tested each group on how many baskets they could score from free throws.

As well as doing what they normally do in training, the players were then given a further instruction. The first group were asked to practice free throws every day for an hour.

The second group were asked to just **visualise** themselves making baskets from free throws for an hour every day.

The third group were not asked to do anything extra.

After 30 days, Dr Biasiotto tested the players again.

The first group who physically practised improved their performance by 24%.

The second group, who visualised themselves making free throws, improved by 23% without touching a basketball.

The third group did not improve which was expected.

Of course those who visualised only were not seeing and wiring in any missed baskets, they were only seeing themselves succeeding each time they made a free throw.

American Psychologist, Andrew Melzoff, tested newborn babies and demonstrated that they can imitate rudimentary manual and facial gestures; the youngest tested being only 41 minutes old. Therefore an innate mechanism must be in place in the newborn's brain that allows such behaviour.

NLP teaches that we have many ways to match other people to improve communication and rapport. Some of the ways we do this are:

Matching physiology - whole or half body, gestures (with care otherwise it becomes mimicry and this will break rapport) and posture such as arms folded or not and legs crossed or not. Is the other person sitting upright, leaning back or leaning forward?

Matching breathing is a powerful way to build rapport and this probably comes from being in the womb and being connected to the mother's breathing and heartbeat.

People who sing in a choir are basically breathing in harmony and they talk about it as an amazing experience and the wonderful feeling it creates. I recently heard a chorister talking on the radio about his experience of singing together with others in a choir as an "overwhelming explosive feeling."

According to a 2013 study from Sweden, human heartbeats synchronise with one another when we sing together.

The key thing to remember about matching is to do this carefully and not mimic others as this will be noticed and will break rapport rather than build it.

We can also match on all the neurological levels (see page 36) and as I said earlier matching does not mean you have to like someone or agree with them or their beliefs. We step into someone else's shoes and world and walk along with them. This matching is called "pacing" and when you do this enough you can encourage others to follow. If they don't follow you go back to pacing (building rapport by matching or acknowledging) and try again until they do follow. First you join with the other person and then lead them and when they follow then this is the **structure of influence**.

When you think about the old man in Terry Dobson's story at the beginning of this book, this is what he did. He chose to ask the drunken man what he had been drinking, not in an accusatory or judgmental way but with a sense of curiosity and interest and he did it in a particular way, a pattern interrupt. He raised his voice to get attention but with a tone of voice that demonstrated his curiosity and interest.

Pattern Interrupt is used in Neuro Linguistic Programming and Hypnosis and is a technique to interrupt and change thought patterns and behaviours. It can be as simple as initiating a handshake and then interrupting that motor skill that ordinarily would be completed; transporting the person into a trance state.

A pattern interrupt takes you to a new place, out of familiar places and routines and into possibility. A pattern can be interrupted by any unexpected question.

Have you ever started to do something and after being interrupted can't remember what it was you were going to do? This confusion state can make you open to suggestion – we are willing to trade our uncomfortable state for another's clarity. A pattern interrupt is also like that moment when someone blends with you in Aikido and you fall into the space created by them entering, moving off the center line, not being there and leading you in a different direction.

It is useful to be able to interrupt your own or someone else's state when stuck in an unresourceful place.

Other ways you can match is in language. By using the other person's words and backtracking you are pacing them and you can then introduce another direction and lead the person, which is influence.

If someone is very angry and loud the worse thing we can say is "calm down." It's a mismatch and won't create rapport and may well escalate the situation.

Try it for yourself. Think of a time you were feeling angry and now hear someone's voice quietly telling you to "Calm Down".

How does that feel for you? Do you think you can instantly switch to being calm and do you feel like you want to?

When someone is angry you can match their words, volume of their voice and energy but at a level just below theirs so as not to escalate the situation. Backtracking or playing back their words is pacing or acknowledging their experience. So it's not just matching the words but also the volume, tone, speed and energy of the voice.

We can match cultures. What we do is always dependent on our outcomes so if you want a job in a bank it's probably best to wear a suit and tie to the interview. By matching we can get ourselves into the communication loop and remember we cannot not communicate whether we are speaking or not. Our presence has an effect and therefore we cannot not influence and by matching and building rapport and being in the communication loop you are open to being influenced yourself.

In Aikido the same principles apply. Who's leading or attacking whom?

Your thoughts, i.e. what you see, hear and feel cause or create feelings that will lead to action and results.

Chapter 8 – Getting In A State

State is the gateway to high performance.

Any performance, be it physical like sports, dance or martial arts will be affected by how we feel as will any other activity like coaching, giving a speech, socialising and learning.

Excellent performance is state dependant.

With elite athletes the difference that makes the difference in their performance is usually in their thinking and mental state and any disruption like anxiety will affect their performance in a negative way. This sort of situation where something unexpected happens and despite your preparation you find yourself unable to deal with whatever has happened. It could mean being interrupted or challenged during a presentation or performance or you receive some negative feedback.

In that moment you need to be able to keep yourself in a good state so that you can continue to make your presentation or perform at your best. One-way to do this is by instantly being able to access good states from the past using what is called, anchors and I will take you through this process on page 226.

I once did some coaching with Brendan Rogers who, at that time was reserve team manager at Chelsea Football Club and number two to Jose Mourinho during his first spell as coach there and now Brendan is Manager at Celtic FC.

Brendan said that he was working with elite athletes who were superbly fit and had amazing ball skills but it was always what their internal state was that made the difference during a game.

An Olympic 100-metre champion athlete had a ritual he performed every time he went out onto the track to run a race. He would stand in his lane, take a few steps down the track and then a few steps back, all the time keeping his eyes on the finish line. Even when a large TV camera was thrust into his face while he was being introduced to the crowd, his gaze would never wander.

Late on in his career he was asked what he was thinking while waiting for the race to begin and he said that he was visualising himself going through the tape first. Every time he saw himself winning he would get the feeling of success. This ritual allowed him to get into a focussed high performance state so that he could explode out of the blocks on the "B of the Bang", as he put it.

A lot of sports people have rituals like this, which are sometimes described as "superstition", but they are in fact "anchors" that stimulate or trigger the focussed state required for high performance.

NLP co-founder, John Grinder, said that there are 3 curses of western civilisation:

1. Excess muscular tension
2. Too much internal dialogue
3. Foveal vision

Better to be relaxed, be quiet on the inside and have soft focus and peripheral vision.

So whatever we are doing it is really useful to have tools and skills to help us get into resourceful positive states so that we can perform at our best and how we feel will be picked up by whomever we are with.

Dumping our problems and negative states on others is not useful so we need tools to be able to choose how we want to feel. We have already talked about the "Getting in the Zone" process and something like anchoring can also be done in a few minutes or less as can self-hypnosis. It is very important to have some tools and daily practice that are available so you can use them easily.

I remember a story I overheard in the pub after training, many years ago when I first started Aikido training. An Aikidoka (Aikido student), a fit, once confident young man was telling the Sensei about something that happened to him which had "destroyed" his self-confidence.

One night when he was travelling home he saw an old lady being mugged on the street and he shouted at the attacker and chased after him.

The mugger ran along the busy street, turned into another street and then disappeared around another corner. The young man chased him around the corner and discovered it was a cul de sac and the mugger was standing in the middle of the road, waiting for him. He came to a halt in front of the mugger and immediately raised his hands in one of those "martial art" stances you see on the movies. The mugger grabbed and twisted his fingers, punched him in the face and ran off leaving him surprised and stunned and with his pride hurt more than his head.

He told Karl Lancaster Sensei that since then all his confidence had gone and whenever something surprised him he would freeze. He asked him:

"What do you recommend I should do?"

The Sensei thought about it for a few minutes and we all waited eagerly in the crowded bar for his words of wisdom. Finally he said:

"Focus on your breathing. When something happens that surprises or scares you and you freeze, put your attention on your breathing."

That's all he said and at that time it didn't mean much to me but I soon had good reason to be grateful for those few words.

A few months later I was lying in bed asleep when I was suddenly awakened by loud angry voices. It was two in the morning and at first I thought it was my young sons fighting but then I recognised my Landlord's voice saying:

"Put the knife down". There was some desperation in his voice and more scuffling on the landing directly outside my sons' bedroom followed this.

Suddenly I was terrified and the feeling was so overwhelming I couldn't move. I lay on my back and could hear and feel my heart pounding. It felt like a scene from a cartoon where you could see my heart going up and down under the sheet.

I was so scared because of concern for my young sons and the angry voices may also have triggered a childhood memory pushing me into a fearful state; either way I had to do something and then I remembered the Sensei's words.

"Focus on your breathing".

So I did. I lay there making my breathing deeper and gradually slowing it down and very soon I could move. I was still scared but I could move and was able to get up and out of my bedroom. As I went down the stairs to the landing I could see my landlord struggling with a man who was holding a knife. He was holding the mans wrist up in the air and as the man saw me coming he managed to free his hand that was holding the knife and I immediately pushed the attacker backwards down the stairs, a well-known Aikido technique!

"Breathe. Let go. And remind yourself that this very moment is the only one you know you have for sure." – Oprah Winfrey

This is an example of our basic survival strategy of fight, flight or freeze which and in an emergency situation we will automatically and immediately be put into one of these positions. Adrenaline floods the system and blood flow to internal organs is reduced and redirected to our muscles to aid our escape or fight. When we freeze we literally stop breathing so that the moment of fear is "frozen" in our physiology and neurology and later can get "triggered" by other threatening events.

In the case of my friend his apparent loss of confidence was as a result of being in this "frozen" state and by consciously focussing on his breathing he was able to put his body back into action. These sorts of "traumas" can create tension that can be held in your muscles and cells and can be triggered by events that surprise or scare you.

In my own case that was certainly true for me and by consciously and purposefully practising putting my attention on my breathing during times when I am surprised or potentially frightened by something I am able to move and take some sort of action. In the martial arts they say the best technique is not to be there so running (flight) is certainly a good option.

A friend called me up and told me about his fear of going to the dentist and how his body felt "numb" at the thought of it. I told him this story about "focussing on his breathing" and he felt OK enough to go to his appointment.

Afterwards he told me about the realisation he had while in the dentist's chair. As a child, while a dentist was cleaning plaque off his teeth the instrument slipped and pierced his gum. It wasn't a serious injury but the surprise of the pain caused him to stiffen and hold his breath in anticipation of more pain and being a child he never thought it was OK to tell the Dentist to stop.

So on this occasion he explained the situation to the dentist who gave him explicit permission to say stop at any time and my friend also practised keeping his breathing going which is of course part of any good meditation practice.

The Dentist said he noticed the patient relaxing during the session and my friend said the numbness in his body and legs disappeared while he was walking home.

Taking a few deep breaths in any fearful situation will stimulate the vagus nerve the "rest-and-digest" aspects of the parasympathetic nervous system. This relaxation response unclamps the neurobiological grip of fear and allows us to "unfreeze" and move freely.

There are also other ways to access useful states. For an Aikidoka, whether they are aware of it consciously or not, standing in hanmi will immediately evoke the mental states achieved on the mat in the dojo which are a state of calmness and relaxation while also being alert, centred and ready to move.

Someone once modelled me on a NLP course because they thought I had a sense of calmness and stillness and they wanted to learn how to get that state for themselves. I chose the context of Aikido training as an example of times when I knew I had that state.

This was an interesting exercise for me because I wasn't aware of what I was doing to get this state and what the modellers found out was that the mostly unconscious strategy I was using started in the changing room. I never chatted very much when I was changing into my gi (martial art training suit) and we discovered that dressing and tying myself in to my hakama was a ritual that began the process of becoming focussed and calm.

Stepping onto the mat and feeling its coolness on the soles of my bare feet, seeing the brightness of the white walls and finally standing in hanmi completed the process. All of these components had an effect and were anchors or stimuli that elicited the same response, i.e. accessing the state of calmness while also being alert.

Obviously knowing how to do this we can consciously use it as a strategy, which in NLP is called anchoring, at any time to be able to get into useful and resourceful states and you will have your own examples of when you know you can feel calm, relaxed etc.

An anchor, in sailing and boating contexts, is a way of stabilising the vessel, holding it in the same place so the current and wind don't carry it away.

Using an anchor will stabilise your state and keep you in a useful place and able to continue to perform well.

"A good stance and posture reflect a proper state of mind". – The Art of Peace, O Sensei.

Standing in hanmi which stimulates or elicits a certain state is what is known in NLP as an "anchor", a stimulus which always gets the same response and in this case the particular state of stillness and readiness.

Emptiness inside, calmness, stillness and being physically settled and grounded all of which facilitates the ability to respond and move spontaneously from your center.

Sometimes we dither, shuffle, forget things, turn up late, make excuses, blame others, and have reasons to explain our inadequacies and procrastinations like "I haven't got time". An aikidoka colleague calls this "spinning". In the martial arts they say: "The hardest thing is getting yourself there".

We all have different ways of thinking about or coding time that can either help us or stop us from doing activities like planning, motivating ourselves to do things we have to do or we want to do.

A friend of mine told me about a university department head, a professor, that he needed to meet with to discuss and plan a piece of work he was going to be employed to present in the near future.

Every time he spoke to him or tried to speak to him on the phone he was rebuffed with the phrase: "I can't speak to you now. I've got no time".

So eventually my friend went to the university campus in an attempt to meet with the professor. He found him and tried to talk to him but received the same message: "I can't talk to you now, I've got no time and need to get back to my office".

"Well do you mind if I walk with you and we can talk on the way?"

"Yes that's OK". Replied the professor and they walked together across the campus chatting all the way and when they arrived at the professor's office they stood chatting for another 10 minutes and my friend managed to get all the information he required and went on his way. He had intuitively matched and built rapport with the Professor by walking along with him and also matched his way of coding time and dealt with his business "in the moment".

This is an example of someone who is "in time". He is in the moment and cannot perceive of "having time" which would require a "through time" thinking strategy that enables building a pathway that is connected through time which is called planning. He or she may also feel "under pressure" a lot because he is holding a lot of things in his thinking at any one time.

There are all the day to day things we do in our lives as well as work and holding all of this rather than diarising it in a plan causes his perception to be that he has "got no time" other than the moment he is in.

The professor had a real felt sense that he had no time because he was always in the moment and my friend had inadvertently matched his pattern and chatted while they were on the move so the professor had no sense they were using time.

As a result of this matching, enough rapport had been built whereby the professor felt comfortable chatting outside his office for a further 10 minutes, an example of matching and leading. Being "in time" or "in the moment" is good for performance and we need the other strategies like "through time" thinking so that we can plan and prepare.

"In the moment" or "in time" thinking is also useful on the battlefield, sports arena, office or boardroom where there are no excuses, mistakes, explanations, blame and moments to procrastinate while we adjust our position so that we are comfortable and then ready to receive the attack, run the race or meeting. There is no time for redundant body language.

"The readiness is all" as Shakespeare's Hamlet, said.

The readiness he refers to is "death" or acceptance of death as in the fencing duel.

We are there in the moment and that is it. This place and how we strive to be is a special internal state of being in the moment. Sports people call this "being in the zone"; in NLP it is known as "uptime".

Got no time for practice? We just have to take it cos there's never going to be any time.

Excuses are what are found written on tombstones. Anyone who has done the Landmark Forum will remember the idea of "being our word", therefore when you make an arrangement you are not just giving your word but "being your word" and this is on the neurological level of identity, like a code of honour, who you are and woe betide anyone who turned up late on the Landmark trainings.

NLP has provided many ways to access these positive states through both mind and body and anyone can learn to be able to do that at any time. In Aikido we are accessing these states by learning through movement of the body, which creates neuro chemical changes such as the production of the "feel good" endorphins and Serotonin, and we take in and retrieve information from the body. We are also training to be present in the moment, to be mindful and aware.

Richard Bandler refers to these neuro chemicals as "Brain Juice" and he uses many ways to stimulate and provoke his students in order to create production of these "feel good" neuro chemicals.

ANCHORING – DOES THE NAME PAVLOV RING A BELL?

Our world is full of anchors. Remember seeing and hearing the sound of fingernails scraping on a blackboard – firstly how did you remember this? Was it that high-pitched sound of scraping nails or did you see a picture of a blackboard first and was there any other stimulus? What's your response to this question?

Now remember the smell of a rose or your favourite flower, hear a special song or piece of music and what happens when you think about biting into a lemon? Do you start salivating like Pavlov's dog?

Often these sorts of things have the ability to transport us back in time to a place where we first experienced the event as in Prousts *"À la recherche du temps perdu"* – known in English as *"In Search of Lost Time"* and *"Remembrance of Things Past"*

Proust describes how the smell and taste of a lemon tea and a madeleine cake transported him back to a time when he was very young, in such vivid detail that it was as if he was re-experiencing the event again. The event occurred on one of his many visits to see his invalid Aunt in the French village of Combray and Proust described this reactivation as: "Involuntary Memory".

The sense of smell is particularly powerful as it has a more direct route to the brain, a leftover from our early days on earth where it was an essential survival strategy.

Also think of wood smoke and autumn leaves burning, percolating coffee, baking bread, freshly cut grass or a perfume and all the memories they can and do evoke and the feelings that come with them.

The good thing is that we don't have to be at the mercy of negative emotions and we can choose to feel how we want.

What will be most useful to feel in a particular context like an interview, doing a presentation, learning or teaching context, business meetings, social events or a memory?

Being aware of and being able to manage your emotions is a key requisite of excellent leadership and performance and anchoring is a quick and easy way to elicit and fix resourceful states.

Anchoring Exercise

- Choose a state (feeling) that you would like to have more of such as relaxation, confidence, calmness, high performance, learning etc.

- Think of a time when you had this state/feeling and in your mind go back to that time. It is important that you are not seeing yourself in the memory, which is called being in a dissociated state, but experiencing the moment as if you are there now. This is called being associated in that moment and this enables you to re-experience the feeling you had at that time as if you are there right now.

- Use all senses and VAK this situation by taking a look around and see where you are, hear any sounds if there are any and allow yourself to get the feeling of confidence, calmness or whatever feeling you are after. Maybe there are other stimuli like smell and tastes. You can do this with several examples thus strengthening the feeling. This is called stacking anchors.

- When you are sure you are building and experiencing the feeling, stabilise it by holding your forefinger and thumb together. You can use any part of the body but finger and thumb, a knuckle or ear lobe are very precise and can easily be used again to re-access the feeling.

- Hold this anchor, your finger and thumb together, as long as the feeling is growing, preferably for a minimum of 10 seconds and while it's at its peak and be sure to release the anchor, your thumb and forefinger, before the feeling begins to fade.

- Do a little break state to get yourself out of the feeling like moving around or literally shaking your arms and body or simply remember what you had for breakfast or have a chat with a friend.

- Now test your anchor by putting your finger and thumb together again and this will bring back the feeling. The good thing about these anchors is that they can be used anytime anywhere and no one will notice what you are doing and it's free. Use it or lose it and remember to regularly top up your anchors.

Anchors can be set in any of our senses and it is important to use and rebuild them otherwise they may fade. Be aware we are anchors for others and others can be anchors for us. So if you enter a room for a meeting with a scowl on your face this will evoke a certain feeling for those present and they will make meanings about you. Similarly if you enter with a smile this will have a completely different effect.

Think about the effect you want to have on others; how do you want them to feel? If you want them to feel curious about something then be in that state of curiosity when you walk in by thinking about a time you know you were curious about something. You are demonstrating that state and they will pick that up and take it on; and it's great fun to practise and notice the responses you get. Storytellers are good at this and they use words in all sensory channels to evoke responses in the reader or listener.

Anchors are used in advertising and branding by building logos that become so familiar we know what they are immediately. There is one large organisation that used to have three words with its logo but no longer does and people still remember exactly what they were. Just the graphic is used now and "everyone" will instantly know what it is when they see it. Do you know which product I am talking about? You may well be wearing it right now.

Chapter 9 – Power

Power is The Ability to Act or Produce an Effect

Ashby's law of requisite variety states that in order to successfully adapt, achieve or survive, a member of a system requires a minimum amount of flexibility. That amount of flexibility has to be proportional to the variety that member must contend with in the rest of the system.

One of the NLP Presuppositions states that the person in a system with the most flexibility and choices will have the most influence.

Variety is required to regulate variety. A system can be defined as self, body and mind, family, friends, colleagues, businesses, cultures etc.

The opposite of power is dependence and in order to change this we need choices.

In Aikido one of the difficult things to learn to do is let go of your own strength. In the attempt to be powerful we do what we have been taught in early life; that is to be strong by using our muscle strength along with lots of effort. This is OK until we meet someone who is bigger and stronger and then it becomes conflict, a limitation.

"We were taught that it was wrong to attempt to develop or resort to physical strength, as this would impede our ability to learn to apply ki when executing techniques. What we were doing was in

one very real sense an "unlearning" process in that we were reprogramming our bodies and minds to deal with physical reality in a new and more efficient manner."

Koichi Tohei – 10th Dan Aikido Sensei

Josh Waitzkin, a chess Grand Master, and an International Master by age 16 later became a Tai Chi Chuan Push Hands World Champion.

In his book "The Art of Learning" Josh talks about "investment in loss".

He says: "In order to grow we have to give up our current mind set."

To be powerful you need to connect to your own core or centre and operate from there whether it's doing Aikido or something like NLP coaching. By having the ability to choose how you feel and be in these high performing states you can develop more flexibility and operate effectively.

"He who conquers others is strong; he who conquers himself is mighty" – Lao Tzu: philosopher of ancient China

Aikido is designed to deal with multiple attackers. Every technique will have this potential built into it. Saito Sensei used to say that there are no mistakes in Aikido because there will always be another technique available and In order to be able to develop these abilities, which give you choices, you need to spend time learning and building your own flexibility.

Flexibility = Choices

This is personal power and it's useful to remember having only one thing is not a choice, two things is a dilemma, an either/or situation which is usually going from one extreme to another which is polarisation not allowing much discussion, so real choice starts with a minimum of three options.

CENTERING

"Every sturdy tree that towers over human beings owes its existence to a deeply rooted core" – The Art of Peace, O Sensei.

Hara is a Japanese word that has no equivalent in English, while it literally refers to the lower abdomen; the term also has psychological and spiritual connotations in Japanese language and culture. In western culture it is mostly referred to as our "Center".

Physical exercise such as Running, Aikido, Tai Chi, Pilates, Basketball and some other form of moving meditation, cause chemical changes in the brain, producing endorphins; the "feel good" pain-killing chemical and these chemical changes create an altered state that enables you to perform at your best.

Effective and accelerated learning is state dependant and any teacher or instructor who is aware of this can utilise various strategies to influence the students states to enhance their learning abilities, for example the use of metaphor, repetitions, role playing and physical movement.

In Aikido there is a lot of emphasis on being grounded, centred and calm, even in the midst of turmoil, so that your balance cannot be taken. Being extended away from your own centre will cause you to lose your balance.

We can also be disturbed and extended from our centre mentally so that we are not in a useful or resourceful inner state and lose our psychological balance; start worrying, getting stressed by running anxiety patterns and grind ourselves to a halt or place of incompetence.

Being centered or on balance is the goal of Aikido and NLP Coaching and Aikido is good at teaching how to keep your center when you are in conflict. Being centred and congruent is a fundamental skill and a very useful resource state and when you lose your centre and get upset, you begin to lose other resources and work against yourself.

CENTERING EXERCISE

"The Bamboo that bends is stronger than the oak that resists"

You can do the following exercise on your own or you can get a friend to help you.

- Stand as you normally would, without resistance and ask your friend to test your balance and stability by gently pushing you on the shoulder, backwards, forwards and to the sides. Push both shoulders, separately and then together. The idea is not to try and push you over but only to see how easy you move and to check your balance.

- Now stand and allow your head and neck to settle comfortably into your shoulders that are relaxed and your arms can hang loose. Settle your hips downwards, bend your knees slightly and keep your feet about shoulder-width distance apart and lining up with your hips.

- Maintaining your gaze directly in front of you with soft focus as well as noticing your peripheral vision, allow your energy, thoughts and breathing to slowly sink down on the inside to a point just below your navel, your centre or hara and once again ask your friend to test your balance by pushing your shoulders. They should notice a difference and so will you. You will be more difficult to move as if stuck to the ground.

This is not being strong and rigid like an oak tree which, given a forceful enough wind will break or uproot, but more like a Willow or Bamboo tree both of which have flexibility as well as strength. In a strong wind they will bend and touch the ground and then are able to come back to their center.

This is a way of coming back to your centre or core and now that you know how to do it you can practise anytime and it only takes a few minutes to easily access a very useful and resourceful inner state.

When you do this regularly you will notice and feel how much more focused you are and how your sense of being has moved more towards the "happiness" end of the scale.

'Grounded' is when we root our centre to the spot, make ourselves solid and 'stand our ground', whatever force may be acting on us.

'Flow' is when we can move with whatever force comes our way, but we move from our centre and maintain our balance.

I often hear people talking about how stressed they are. They may have busy jobs, families and mortgages to deal with. It could be that they are out of work and worried about the bills. All of this can add up to feeling stressed.

Stress, or feeling stressed, has a structure: we create internal pictures of what is or may go wrong, talk to ourselves in an anxious tone of voice and get a bad feeling. Then we loop around again, doing the same thing, possibly making the pictures more vivid, the internal voice more desperate and then get a more intense bad feeling.

This is the structure of anxiety, causing what you call stress. You need to notice this internal strategy and then interrupt it. Later I have included a piece about how to deal with negative internal dialogue by changing the voice to a cartoon character. Changing your state by getting centered is another way to deal with unwanted feelings.

Some people may protest that there are all of these negative things going on in their life so they have to worry about them and it causes them to feel stressed. Yes of course it is important to deal with the problems and the key here is to be able to maintain a useful positive state and then you will be able to deal with the difficulties in a more effective way. I'm not saying ignore the problem but rather feel better when dealing with it. Remember what Einstein said:

"We can't solve problems by using the same kind of thinking we used when we created them." – Albert Einstein

CENTERING FOR A CHALLENGING SITUATION

When doing this Centering exercise it is useful to stand in different spaces for each step.

1. Remember a time when there was a challenge and it was difficult for you to stay centred – associate into that experience as if it is going on now.
2. Step out of that time and remember a state where you feel relaxed, aligned and centred. Think of an example in your life where you felt like that to help you get that state now.
3. When you are ready, ask you partner to gently push and pull you in different directions while you practise staying centred.
4. As you develop the skill even more ask your partner to increase what they are doing to create more of a challenge and stretch for you.
5. Explore both 'grounding' and 'flowing' this way.
6. When ready step back into the previous challenging situation as in step 1 with this state of being centered and notice and sense how the experience is now different.

Chapter 10 – Joining the Dots

In order to learn a technique we break it down into its component parts and learn to do the first part and then the next part. This is how we learn in the beginning. When I used to teach in Colleges or Universities I would ask students:

"How do you eat an elephant?"

They initially thought it was a weird question but would usually come up with the answer, which is of course:

"A mouthful at a time."

In order to learn anything it is useful to chunk it down into smaller parts and then you can connect each part and build the whole. As a beginner, Aikido techniques can be learnt like this but in order to be effective they must be one integrated movement just like in the four stages of learning when we reach stage 4, unconscious competence. The beginning may facilitate or determine what happens next but they are not disconnected.

Successful completion of an Aikido technique is reliant on the "awase", matching and utilising the opponent's energy and momentum so that they never regain their balance and they are overcome. They are extended off their center and not given any openings and opportunities to regain it.

"Even the most powerful human being has a limited sphere of strength. Draw him outside of his/her sphere and into your own and his strength will dissipate" – The Art of Peace, O Sensei.

An Aikidoka (Aikido student) who is also a guitarist explains how when strumming the strings in a rhythm, the movement is not just up and down but is also in a vertical figure of eight and while making this move the plectrum or fingers can stay in contact with the strings. The seed of the upward stroke is contained in the downward stroke and vice versa. Up and down are connected and it is one integrated movement.

The idea of separate parts happens with us in life and we often talk about parts of ourselves. On the one hand we want to do something and on the other hand we want something else and get stopped. These "parts" are not connected and we develop our own internal conflict where one part wants something and the other part stops you because it wants something else and may also be protecting you in some way, (positive intention).

You may remember George W Bush saying something like this when he was President:

"You're either for me or against me."

That has some negative consequences, not the least of which is a complete loss of dialogue and opportunity to learn.

For example a person may have a part that wants to be spontaneously creative and another part that is risk averse and concerned with spotting problems and avoiding trouble. There is nothing wrong with a healthy sceptic but often in these situations the creative part is stopped because of the other part's sometimes-inappropriate concerns. We are being pulled in two different directions and this can cause a sense of frustration and lack of fulfilment as the person never gets to do what they really want and they usually don't know why.

It's almost as if each part is unaware of the positive side of the other part and what it is trying to achieve, why it is doing what its doing and in order to resolve this conflict you need to get the parts to see and appreciate the resources and positive intention of each other, realise you have a mutual goal because both parts ultimately want success and then it is much easier to begin to negotiate. At some level both parts, or could be people involved in a negotiation, realise they both want the same thing, i.e. success, and it is then a matter of how you can work together to achieve your mutual goal.

Sometimes in an Organisation that is going through a change programme, someone or could be a department or team, dig their heels in and refuse to utilise the new procedures. In those circumstances there is always a positive intention for that person or department at that time, some sort of benefit they get from the existing procedures and the fear of losing those benefits will cause them to dig in. When the positive intention is addressed they can begin to move forward.

Pace or acknowledge each part and find out the positive intention behind the situation, ask what each person or part gets from not changing or agreeing. Ask why the part is behaving like that, what does that behaviour get for them.

There are situations where you may be physically or mentally held and pulled in opposite directions by two people. Obviously using strength and pulling against them both is probably not going to work, however when we use Aikido principles and match one side by shifting our centre towards that person we can then align ourselves with them and now it is two of us pulling in the same direction and we are able to draw the other person along. From that position there are then techniques that can be done.

Remember in any successful negotiation you need to build rapport with each side so as to bring them together as in the physical example above and also utilise strategies and resources to achieve a win/win so that neither part lose anything.

Find out the specific information about the current situation of both parts.

What's the positive intention behind the current behaviour i.e. being in conflict?

What do they want?

Chunk up to find the mutual goal. You can do this by asking:

What's important to you about achieving this goal, what does that do for you?

It is useful to connect the parts so that they are aware of the resources each has and then build a mutual outcome. As parts they operate at extremes from each other and have no access to the resources of the other, they are disconnected.

Ask each part, or person if you are working with others, what their outcome is and then ask what that outcome achieves for them and for what purpose do they want that?

We can also apply these questions to ourselves and perhaps we should. Coaching requires that you know yourself first and from that platform you can help others know themselves.

If you are working on your own internal conflict it's necessary to be operating from a Meta position, i.e. put the parts out in front of you and direct the questions to each part separately.

At some level the parts will want the same thing, such as success, and when each part becomes aware that the other part is working on your behalf a successful negotiation can then bring the parts together so that they are one self-regulating integrated system and then all the abilities, choices and resources are always available and this ties in with Ashby's Law of Requisite Variety, as previously mentioned.

This is like inner team building and a team working together can create something that the parts can't or won't be able to do on its own, whether it's people or parts of our selves.

"Two Wolves" is a Cherokee Indian legend:

An old Cherokee is teaching his grandson about life. "A fight is going on inside me," he said to the boy.

"It is a terrible fight and it is between two wolves. One is evil – he is anger, envy, sorrow, regret, greed, arrogance, self-pity, guilt, resentment, inferiority, lies, false pride, superiority, and ego." He continued, "The other is good – he is joy, peace, love, hope, serenity, humility, kindness, benevolence, empathy, generosity, truth, compassion, and faith. The same fight is going on inside you – and inside every other person, too."

The grandson thought about it for a minute and then asked his grandfather, "Which wolf will win?"

The old Cherokee simply replied, "The one you feed."

Pattern learning and the importance of relationship

Gregory Bateson received a government grant to study Dolphin behaviour especially in relation to how they are trained and he went to the Marine Research Institute in Hawaii where he worked with the instructors while they taught the dolphins to perform in public shows.

The process started with an untrained dolphin and these days only dolphins born in captivity are used. During the first day, when the dolphin did something different, like jumping outside the water, the instructor blew a whistle and, as a reward, gave the dolphin a fish.

Whenever the dolphin behaved that way, the instructor used the whistle and threw it a fish. Soon, the dolphin learned that its behaviour guaranteed it a fish; it repeated the behaviour continually, always waiting for and getting a reward.

The next day, the dolphin was let into the tank where it performed its jump and waited for a fish. It got nothing. For some time, the dolphin repeated its jump but got no reward.

Eventually it tried some other behaviour, like a turn. The instructor then blew the whistle and gave it a fish. Whenever the dolphin repeated the new piece of acrobatics, in the same session, it received the reward of a fish. No fish for the prowess of yesterday, only for something new.

This pattern was repeated for 14 days. The dolphin swam in to the tank and repeated the behaviours that it had learned and performed in the previous day, without any reward. Many times, the dolphin performed some of its acrobatics of the previous days, without any further reward and it only received a fish when it did something new.

Probably that was frustrating for the dolphin. However, on the fifteenth day, suddenly, it appeared to have learned the rules of the game and stepped up the levels of learning. It got animated and introduced a surprising show, including eight new and different behaviours, four of which had never been observed before in the species.

The dolphin appeared to have comprehended not just how to generate a new behaviour, but also the rules about how and when to generate them. The little dolphins are intelligent.

A last detail: during the 14 days Bateson noted that the instructor threw fishes to the dolphin away from the training context. Bateson became curious and questioned this attitude. The instructor answered: "Oh that is to keep them on friendly terms, naturally.

After all, if we don't have a good relationship they will get bored and will not bother about learning and showing something new".

So whatever we are doing where we need to take people with us, knowing how to build rapport becomes an invaluable tool.

The NLP model of leadership is building a community that other people want to belong to so we sort of draw others along with us and that is also what we are attempting to do in Aikido, isn't it?

"All I know is I know nothing" – Socrates

This is the state we need in modelling, the "know nothing state" so that we are open and do not impose our own ideas on what we think the exemplar is doing. It is like what Chiba Shihan calls "Beginners Mind".

Kazuo Chiba Shihan who was born February 5, 1940 passed away on June 5, 2015. He was a Japanese Aikido teacher and founder of Birankai International. He served for seven years as uchideshi at the Aikikai Hombu Dojo in Tokyo where he trained under Kisshomaru Ueshiba, the son of the Aikido founder and he accompanied O Sensei on his teaching travels around Japan, before being dispatched abroad to help develop Aikido internationally. He held an 8th dan in Aikido, issued by Aikikai world headquarters in Tokyo, Japan and was active in Aikido for over 50 years.

He was asked in an interview in 2015 what his message to his students and other Aikidoists would be. Here is what he said:

"My message to future Aikidoists or present practitioners... Is to keep up your Shoshin. Shoshin is Beginner's Mind. Shoshin is, if I may say, unstained mind. Preconceptual mind. Whenever you come on the mat, not necessarily on the mat, but because the mat is where our center of training is expressed, I say on the mat. You must clarify your own motivation, right from the bottom. Clear up, Purify. Sit there and wait for instruction with unstained mind. That has to be continuously carried out throughout your Aikido life. Whatever rank you may attain, does not really make a difference. Always go down to the bottom with heart, and check your Shoshin all the time".

"In the beginner's mind there are many possibilities, in the expert's there are few." – Shunryu Suzuki-roshi

The more I see contemporary senior Sensei and Shihan in action, the more I realise how much more there is for me to learn as Chiba Shihan said in his message.

According to Andy Hathaway Sensei this was always emphasised by Morihiro Saito Shihan, who spent all his life preserving the original Aikido of O-Sensei. He said:

"When we are lost in our Aikido always return to the base"

Those people with a "moving away from" motivation pattern say that the devil is in the detail and I like to think that God is in the detail and more than that in the detail of the basics. The basics are like a capsule containing all the principles of Aikido.

Conclusion

Aikido and NLP have now developed, expanded and split into many different styles.

Courses advertised as NLP often include a lot of other material and though that other material may be effective in its own right, it is not NLP or NLP Applications.

Some of the different Aikido styles bear little resemblance to Budo but could be described as gymnastic dance and requires fitness and skill but it is not martial or Budo. It is only when we are training as if it is combat and attacks are made with a proper attitude that we can truly learn the difference that makes the difference that enables us to succeed and that is in the detail of the basics and is therefore not a detail.

Traditional Iwama Aikido:

"Aikido is generally believed to represent circular movements. Contrary to such beliefs, however, Aikido, in its true ki form, is a fierce art, piercing straight through the center of the opposition." – Morihiro Saito Shihan

The heart of NLP is modelling and from modelling comes NLP applications which can be used to, as Richard Bandler says:

"Help people think on purpose so you can change the way you think which will change the way you feel and therefore what you can do, and people like stuff that works".

And from John Grinder:

"The only justification for the application of NLP Patterns is the creation of choice in precisely those sets of contexts where choice presently does not exist. Ask, 'What's missing here? What does this person not have that if they had it would make a difference to their seeking?" – John Grinder

So what do we do now or how would someone new to these disciplines choose a teacher?

You can usually find an Aikido Dojo local to where you live by searching on the Internet. A good teacher will strive to teach the material that goes back to the founder, O Sensei.

Many NLP processes use visualisation of future successful events so ask "What will I be in 10 years if I join this school," rather than asking "Which teacher can make me the best fighter in the least amount of time?"

Apart from my first few years of Aikido training I have always trained in what is known as Iwama style. Iwama is where O Sensei and Saito Shihan were based and taught. Many Japanese and western students studied there and brought their learnings to the West.

Do some research and find NLP trainers who run courses that teach the basics and the art of modelling and tell good stories. After all the most advanced techniques won't work without the basics.

According to Andy Hathaway Sensei the "basics" is a capsule in which all the principles of Aikido are encapsulated.

BACK TO BASICS

Once upon a time there was a very wise old teacher who was addressing a group of students somewhere in the Orient.

On the floor to the left of his chair was a pile of rocks, to his right were several boxes and on the floor in front of him was a large glass jar. I think it is called a Bell Jar.

The old man picked up a rock and carefully placed it inside the jar. Then he picked up another rock, placed it carefully inside the jar and another and another until he couldn't get any more rocks in the jar.

He paused, stroked his long white beard and then asked the group:

"Is the jar now full?"

Lots of hands went up and all the students shouted:

"Yes the jar is full?"

He smiled and said:

"Oh no its not".

Then he leaned over, placed his hand in one of the boxes and lifted out a pile of small pebbles that he carefully dropped into the jar so they trickled down between the rocks until he couldn't get any more in.

"Is the jar now full?" he asked the group.

"Yes it is". A few students replied.

Once again the old teacher smiled and said:

"Oh no its not".

Then he placed his hand inside another box and brought out a handful of sand which he poured into the jar and then another until he couldn't get any more in.

He looked at the group again, smiled and asked:

"Is the jar now full?"

There was a pause and then two students put their hands up and said:

"Yes the jar is now full".

The teacher smiled and said:

"Oh no its not full".

Then he reached under his chair and brought out a jug full of water that he carefully poured into the jar until slowly it reached the top.

He looked up, smiled and asked:

Is the jar now full?

There was a long pause and then one brave student put up his hand and said:

"Yes the jar is full to the top and you can't get any more in there".

The teacher, serious now, looked at the group and then after a while he put his hand in his pocket and brought out a small paper packet that was twisted together at the top. He carefully untwisted the paper revealing a little pile of salt.

Slowly he poured the salt into the jar until eventually a small bump formed at the surface of the water in the jar and once again he asked the group:

"Is the jar now full?"

There was a long silence until one brave student shouted out:

"No the jar is not full"

The teacher immediately replied:

"Ah but yes it is full to the top now and we can't get any more of anything in there".

Then he looked at the group, smiled, slowly stroked his long white beard again and said:

"We have put many things in the jar and it is now full and there are probably many meanings you can make about this demonstration, and remember this". He paused dramatically, raised his finger and said:

"ALWAYS PUT YOUR ROCKS IN FIRST"

This story comes from Steven Covey and I got it in this form from Nick Owen. Judy DeLozier says it's probably a Sufi story and that most stories come from Sufi tradition.

CHAPTER 11 – CURIOSITY

It was my intention to "trigger" your sense of curiosity and anticipation at the beginning of this book as to what it is about and what's coming up later. I don't know how curious you are now, looking back, about how I did that but I do know your curiosity is essential for learning and motivates you to take a step into new and unfamiliar territory knowing it can get uncomfortable sometimes as you strive to make it more familiar and slowly but surely wire in new ways, new habits and learn to be curious rather than feeling upset or embarrassed about your errors and mistakes for that is where the information resides that will guide your next steps as you continue to fill the knowledge gaps and that enables you to make all the necessary adjustments in what you are doing to incrementally improve.

How do you motivate yourself to be curious? What do you see, hear and feel to either, get yourself to stop or put off and avoid doing something or to get yourself to get going after something you want.

As Tony Robbins says:

"Life is the dance between what you fear most and what you desire most".

The Internet and particularly Google have given us the ability to get information and find the answers to questions and solve problems pretty much instantly and we no longer need to exercise our brains in search of answers.

Writer, Ian Leslie in his book "Curious" says the following:

"By supplying answers to questions with such ruthless efficiency, the Internet cuts off the supply of an even more valuable commodity: productive frustration. Education, at least as I remember it, isn't only, or even primarily, about creating children who are proficient with information. It's about filling them with questions that ripen, via deferral, into genuine interests."

Perhaps this is what happens to Aikidoka. The drop out rate in Aikido is huge for all sorts of reasons but the students who do continue reach a point where they have acquired some knowledge and then get fascinated by the learning process.

They have learnt, mostly by practice, a certain amount of information and now want to know more and you see other more experienced students performing techniques and you want to know what it is those students are doing.

They sort of get addicted to wanting to learn more. Knowledge drives curiosity.

The more knowledge you have, the more you are curious to find out more. It's an on-going process, it doesn't finish, just more knowledge and more…

Tony Buzan in his book: "The Mindmapping Book" talks about how the human brain is always looking for completeness, it wants to know the whole thing, the

Gestalt, the idea that natural systems and their properties should be viewed as wholes, not as collections of parts.

Outside the Aikido Club and off the mat you'll see Aikidoka in the pub after training, and I certainly do this, borrowing someone's arm and wrist so they can practice nikyo or sankyo technique and share information about how they work. They have had a taste of being able or nearly able to do a technique and have seen the Sensei demonstrating and explaining how to do it and they are after the details, the difference that makes the difference, and can't wait for the next class and so they continue to investigate in the pub which is always a good place to exchange information.

I also used to do this when I was learning and assisting on NLP Master Practitioner courses. We would spend evenings in the bar practicing techniques, language patterns and eliciting hypnotic trance states in each other, sometimes covertly.

On a recent after-aikido training visit to the Pub, The Rochester Castle, once a venue on the London Pub Rock circuit during the 1970s and now a Wetherspoon Pub in Stoke Newington High Street, I witnessed an interesting scene. Our Aikido class finished at 10pm and it was about 10.30pm by the time we got to the pub.

There were three of us, The Sensei, a long-term student and myself. While we were enjoying our drink after a good training session, the Sensei asked the other student how her extra training for her 2nd Dan grading was going and he asked her if there was anything she needed help with.

She talked about a particular move she wasn't sure of and the Sensei explained that it was about how you blended with the other person and instead of taking hold of their hand you stroked down their forearm with your hand using kokyu, in a particular way while at the same time adding weight to it. He began to demonstrate the move across the table, avoiding the glasses of beer and showing the difference between the affect of the incorrect way compared to the correct way to connect, how that point makes taking their balance more effective, the difference that makes the difference.

It's so subtle that you would never detect it while watching a demonstration unless you were very experienced and even then I've seen a lot of experienced people who are not aware of this point. I have been making these after-training visits to the pub for over 30 years and it is when and where I have learnt a lot of "imperceptible points".

We finished our beer and moved outside the busy pub. It was after midnight and the street was still busy and I said goodnight and went along the road to my car. As I got into the car I looked back and saw, about 50 yards away, silhouetted by car headlamps and the orange cast of the street lights, 2 shadowy figures moving on the pavement, connected to each other. In the gloom I saw the shape of the Sensei and his student practicing Aikido. He was showing her the move that we had talked about in the pub. I could still see the fading image of them in my rear view mirrors as I drove away and I couldn't help smiling.

No time like the present especially when you are doing what you are passionate about.

"A journey of a thousand miles begins with a single step." – Lao-tzu

"The Art of Peace begins with you. Work on yourself and your appointed task in the Art of Peace. Everyone has a spirit that can be refined, a body that can be trained in some manner, a suitable path to follow. You are here for no other purpose than to realise your inner divinity and manifest your inner enlightenment. Foster peace in your own life and then apply the Art to all that you encounter." – The Art of Peace, Morihei Ueshiba (O Sensei)

O Sensei

REFERENCES

Aikido Journal – https://www.aikidojournal.com

Akira Kurosawa – (1910–1998) was a Japanese film director, producer, screenwriter and editor. Regarded as one of the most important and influential filmmakers in the history of cinema, Kurosawa directed 30 films in a career spanning 57 years.

Albert Mehrabian – (born 1938 in an Armenian family in Iran, currently Professor Emeritus of Psychology, UCLA) has become known best by his publications on the relative importance of verbal and nonverbal messages. His findings on inconsistent messages of feelings and attitudes have been quoted throughout human communication seminars worldwide, and have also become known as the 7%–38%–55% rule.

Alvin Toffler – (born October 4, 1928) is an American writer and futurist, known for his works discussing the digital revolution, communication revolution and technological singularity.

Dr Anders K Ericsson – (born 1947) is a Swedish psychologist and Conradi Eminent Scholar and Professor of Psychology at Florida State University who is widely recognized as one of the world's leading theoretical and experimental researchers on expertise.

Ericsson (1990) says that it takes 10,000 hours (20 hours for 50 weeks a year for ten years = 10,000) to become an expert in almost anything and his on-going investigation into genius of all kinds reveals the process of deliberate practice.

Andrew N. Meltzoff – (born February 9, 1950) is an American psychologist and an internationally recognized expert on infant and child development. His discoveries about infant imitation greatly advanced the scientific understanding of early cognition, personality and brain development.

Art of Peace – Morihei Ueshiba, (1883–1969) founder of Aikido and known as "O Sensei" meaning Master or Great Teacher.

Art of War – ancient Chinese military treatise that is attributed to Sun Tzu a high ranking military general and strategist of the Kingdom of Wu who was active in the late sixth century BC. Composed of 13 chapters, each of which is devoted to one aspect of warfare, it is said to be the definitive work on military strategies and tactics of its time, and is still read for its military insights.

Bruce Lee / Lee Jun-fan – (1940–1973) known professionally as Bruce Lee, was a Hong Kong and American actor, Martial Artist, Philosopher, filmmaker, and founder of the martial art Jeet Kune Do..

Budo – Book of techniques and teachings of the Founder of Aikido by Morihei Ueshiba (O Sensei), Kisshomaru Ueshiba and John Stevens.

Carl Gustav Jung – (1875–1961) was a Swiss psychotherapist and psychiatrist who founded analytical psychology. Jung proposed and developed the concepts of the extraverted and the introverted personality archetypes, and the collective unconscious. His work has been influential in psychiatry and in the study of religion, literature and related fields.

Carl Rogers – (1902–1987) was an influential American psychologist and among the founders of the humanistic approach to psychology.

Charles Faulkner – (born 12 January 1952) is a master NLP Practitioner and Master Trainer, Life Coach, motivational speaker, trader and author.

Faulkner developed Neuro-linguistic Programming methods of modelling excellence in the world of finance. He has authored a number of books and audio tapes, of which the most well-known audio is "NLP: The New Technology of Achievement." Jack D Schwager profiles Faulkner in the book "The New Market Wizards".

Chris Evans – Radio DJ and TV Presenter.

Christopher Logue, CBE - (23 November 1926 – 2 December 2011) was an English poet associated with the British Poetry Revival and a pacifist.

Daniel Jay Goleman – (born March 7 1946) is an author, psychologist and science journalist. He is the author of more than 10 books on psychology, education, science and leadership.

Goleman wrote the internationally best-selling book, "Emotional Intelligence" (1995 Bantam Books) that spent more than one and a half years on the New York Times Best Seller List.

Eckhart Tolle – (born 1948) is a spiritual teacher and best selling author. A German-born Canadian resident, he is the author of "The Power of Now" and "A New Earth".

Eric Hoffer (1902–1983) was an American social writer. He was the author of ten books and was awarded the Presidential Medal of Freedom in February 1983.

George Miller – American psychologist who wrote "The Magical Number Seven, Plus or Minus Two: Some Limits on Our Capacity for Processing Information." Originally published in The Psychological Review, 1956, vol. 63, pp. 81–97 and generally known as "Miller's Law".

Recent research has demonstrated that not only is the law based on a misinterpretation of Miller's paper, but that the correct number is probably around three or four bits of information.

Gregory Bateson – (1904–1980) was an English anthropologist, social scientist, linguist, visual anthropologist, semiotician and cyberneticist whose work intersected that of many other fields.

Hank Williams – (1923–1953) was an American singer-songwriter and musician. Regarded as one of the most significant and influential American singers and songwriters of the 20th century, William's recorded 35 singles (five released posthumously) that reached the Top 10 of the *Billboard* Country & Western Best Sellers chart, including 11 that ranked number one (three posthumously).

Williams died in 1953 at the age of 29, from heart failure exacerbated by pills and alcohol.

Ian Leslie – (1926–2011) He was a playwright and screenwriter as well as a film actor. His screenplays were *Savage Messiah* and *The End of Arthur's Marriage*. He was a long-term contributor to *Private Eye* magazine, as well as writing for Alexander Trochi's literary journal, *Merlin*.

Angela Isadora Duncan – (1877–1927) was a dancer, considered by many to be the creator of modern dance. Duncan had many lovers and bore two children, Deirdre (born September 24, 1906), by theatre designer, Craig Gordon, and Patrick (born 1 May 1910), by Paris Singer; both children drowned in a car accident on the Seine River on 19 April 1913, and Duncan herself died years later in another when her long scarf caught in the tires of an automobile in which she was riding, breaking her neck.

James Clear – Entrepreneur, Author in Durham, North Carolina and writes about health, Wellness and Fitness.

Joe Simpson – (born 1960) is an English mountaineer, author and motivational speaker. He is best known for his book "Touching the Void" and the 2003 film adaptation of this epic tale of his survival after a fall in the Peruvian mountains.

John Grinder – John Grinder, Ph.D., born Jan. 10, 1940 is an American linguist, author, management consultant, trainer and speaker. Grinder is credited with the co-creation with Richard Bandler of the field of Neuro-Linguistic Programming.

John Lilly (Dr) – (January 6, 1915 – September 30, 2001) was an American physician, neuroscientist, psychoanalyst, psychonaut, philosopher, writer and inventor.

He was a researcher of the nature of consciousness using mainly isolation tanks, dolphin communication, and psychedelic drugs sometimes in combination.

http://67.55.50.201/lilly/index.html

Joshua Waitzkin – (born December 4, 1976) is an American chess player, martial arts competitor, USA and World Tai Chi Push Hands Champion and author of two books. As a child, he was recognized as a prodigy, and won the U.S. Junior Chess championship in 1993 and 1994. He is the only person to have won the National Primary, Elementary, Junior High School, High School, U.S. Cadet, and U.S. Junior Closed chess championships in his career. The movie "Searching for Bobby Fischer" is based on his early life.

In his second book – *The Art of Learning: An Inner Journey to Optimal Performance* (2008), Waitzkin recounts the story of his years as a chess competitor from his own perspective. He describes how movie fame challenged his concentration on the game, how he took up Tai Chi as a form of relaxation, and then discovered that the same learning techniques he employed in chess enabled him to advance rapidly in martial arts as well. He subsequently studied eastern philosophies and the psychology of learning.

Judith DeLozier – is a trainer and author in NLP. Her interests are in culture, anthropology and Gregory Bateson's epistemology.

A member of Grinder & Bandler's original group of students, she continues to contribute extensively to the development of NLP models and processes. Co-author of "Turtles All The Way Down; Prerequisites to Personal Genius" 1986 and "The Encylopedia of Systemic NLP and New Coding" in 2000 with Robert Dilts.

Julian Russell – Executive Coach and author and owner of PPD Consulting which offers Professional Training & Coaching.

Karl Lancaster – First Aid Trainer and Martial Arts Coach, Author and antiques dealer

Between 2005 and 2007 was double gold medallist and British Champion, also European Champion and in 2010 became World Champion in Kung Fu.

Landmark Education – offers The Landmark Forum, graduate courses, and seminars in the field of personal development.

Lao Tzu – was an ancient Chinese Philosopher and writer. He is known as the reputed author of the Tao Te Ching and the founder of philosophical Taoism, and as a deity in religious Taoism and Traditional Chinese Religions. Although a legendary figure, he is usually dated to around the 6th century BC and reckoned to be a contemporary of Confucius.

Michael Field – is the head full time professional instructor at Field Aikido, based in Melbourne. Michael Field Sensei studied Aikido under Morihiro Saito Sensei 9th Dan Aikikai, while living in Japan at the Iwama Dojo

1979 – 1982, April 1987, April 1994, April/May 1995, July 1996 & March 1999.

He helped bring Saito Sensei to Australia to give Iwama Ryu Aikido Seminars on ten occasions and also hosted Hitohiro Saito Sensei to Melbourne twice, Saburo Takayasu Sensei four times, Hiroki Nemoto Sensei twice and Ulf Evenas Sensei five times.

Michael Grinder – is a master of, and world-renown expert in non-verbal communication, non-verbal leadership, group dynamics, advanced relationship building skills and presentation skills.

Marco Iacoboni – Neurologist and neuro scientist and currently director of the Transcranial Magnetic Stimulation Laboratory at the Ahmanson-Lovelace Brain Mapping Centre UCLA and is the author of "Mirroring People".

Marshall McLuhan – (1911–1980) was a Canadian philosopher of communication theory. His work is viewed as one of the cornerstones of the study of media theory, as well as having practical applications in the advertising and television industries.

Martin E. P. "Marty" Seligman (born August 12, 1942) is an American psychologist, educator, and author of self-help books. Since the late 90's, Seligman has been an avid promoter within the scientific community for the field of positive psychology. His theory of learned helplessness is popular among scientific and clinical psychologists. A review of a General Psychology survey, published in 2002, ranked Seligman as the 31st most cited psychologist of the 20th century.

Matthew Syed – (born 2nd November 1970) is a British journalist, author and broadcaster. He has worked for The Times newspaper since 1999. He has published two books, *Bounce* in 2010, and *Black Box Thinking* in 2015.

Miles Dewey Davis III – (May 26, 1926 – September 28, 1991) was an American jazz musician, bandleader, and composer. Widely considered one of the most influential and innovative musicians of the 20th century, Davis was, together with his musical groups, at the forefront of several major developments in jazz music, including bebop, cool jazz, third stream, modal jazz, post bop and jazz fusion.

In 2008, his 1959 album "Kind of Blue" received its fourth platinum certification from the Recording Industry Association of America.

Milton Hyland Erickson – (5 December 1901 in Aurum Nevada – 25 March 1980 in Phoenix, Arizona) was an American psychiatrist specializing in medical hypnosis and family therapy. He is noted for his approach to the unconscious mind as creative and solution-generating. He is also noted for influencing brief therapy, strategic family therapy, family systems therapy and solution focused brief therapy, and neuro-linguistic programming.

Ericksonian Hypnosis is a method of indirect hypnosis named after Dr. Milton Erickson. A prominent American psychiatrist and psychologist, Erickson is widely regarded as the "father of hypnotherapy".

Dr. Erickson found that **indirect suggestion** could result in therapeutic behavioural change. He preferred to converse with clients using metaphors, contradictions, symbols, and antidotes to influence their behaviour rather than direct orders.

Miyamoto Musashi – (c. 1584–1645), also known as Shinmen Takezō, Miyamoto Bennosuke, or by his Buddhist name Niten Dōraku, was a Japanese swordsman and Samurai. Author of "The Book of Five Rings".

Nick Owen – Consultant, NLP Trainer & Author of "Magic of Metaphor".

Norman Cousins – (June 24, 1915 – November 30, 1990) was an American political journalist, author, professor, and world peace advocate.

He was the author of: *Anatomy of an Illness as Perceived by the Patient: Reflections on Healing*

O. Fred Donaldson, Ph.D. – is a play specialist internationally recognized for his on-going research and use of play with children and animals for forty years. He has coined the term "original play" to describe his work.

O Sensei – Morihei Ueshiba (December 14, 1883 – April 26, 1969) was a famous martial artist and founder of the japanes martial art of Aikido. He is often referred to as "the founder" Kaiso or O Sensei, "Great Teacher".

Peter Gray – Research Professor, Department of Psychology, Boston College and known as an evolutionary psychologist. Author of *Free to Learn: Why Unleashing the Instinct to Play Will Make Our Children Happier, More Self-Reliant, and Better Students for Life* (Basic Books, 2013)

Richard Bandler – Dr Richard Wayne Bandler (born February 24, 1950) is an American author and trainer in the fields of alternative psychology and of self-help. He is best known as the co-inventor (with John Grinder) of Neuro-linguistic programming (NLP), a collection of concepts and techniques intended to understand and change human behavior-patterns. He also developed other systems known as Design Human Engineering® (DHE®) and Neuro Hypnotic Repatterning™ (NHR™).

Rick Hanson, Ph. D. – Psychologist, Senior Fellow of the Greater Good Science Center at UC Berkeley and New York Times best-selling author. His books include: Hard wiring Happiness (in 14 languages), Buddha's Brain (in 25 languages), Just one Thing (in 14 languages) and Mother Nurture.

Riki Moss – Sculptor born and raised in Brooklyn. NY. BA University of Chicago, MFA Vermont College of Fine Arts, Studies at the San Francisco Art Institute, New School for Social Research and the University of Vermont.

Rintu Basu – NLP Trainer & Hypnotist www.thenlpcompany.com

Robert Beno Cialdini – (born April 27, 1945) is the Regent's Professor Emeritus of Psychology and Marketing at Arizona State University and was a visiting professor of marketing, business and psychology at Stanford University, as well as at the University of California at Santa Cruz. He is best known for his 1984 book on persuasion and marketing, *Influence: The Psychology of Persuasion*.

Robert Dilts – (born 1955) has been a developer, author, trainer and consultant in the field of Neuro Linguistic Programming (NLP) since its creation in 1975 by John Grinder and Richard Bandler. Dilts has made many personal contributions to the field of NLP including the co-authorship of the Encyclopedia of Systemic NLP. He is best known for his work on beliefs and strategies. www.nlpu.com

Saito Shihan – Morihiro Saito (March 31, 1928 – May 13, 2002) was a teacher of the Japanese martial art of aikido, with many students around the world. Saito's practice of aikido spanned 56 years, from the age of 18, when he first met aikido founder Morihei Ueshiba, until his death in 2002.

Shunryu Suzuki-roshi – (1904–1971) was a Zen Monk and Teacher who helped popularise Zen Buddhism in the United States, and is renowned for founding the first Buddhist Monastery outside Asia, Tassajara Zen Mountain Centre. A book of his teachings, Zen Mind, Beginner's Mind, is one of the most popular books on Zen and Buddhism in the West.

Simon Horton – Author of "Negotiation Mastery", Trainer and Consultant.

Stephen Covey – (1932 – July 2012) was an American educator, author, businessman and keynote speaker. His most popular book was "The Seven Habits of Highly Effective People".

He was a professor at the Jon M Huntsman School of Business at Utah State University at the time of his death.

Stephen G Gilligan Ph.D. – (born Dec. 26th, 1954) is an American author, registered psychologist, psychotherapist and author, Gilligan was selected as one of the first students and developers of the work of Milton H Erickson, considered the founder of modern hypnotherapy. Ni Dan (2nd Dan) Aikido Yudansha.

Sue Knight – international consultant and author pioneering the use of NLP in leadership in business. www.sueknight.co.uk

The Book of Five Rings – is a text on kenjutsu and the martial arts in general, written by the samurai warrior Miyamoto Musashi, circa 1645. It is considered a classic treatise on military strategy, much like Sun Tzu's The Art of War.

The London Aikido Club –
www.londonaikidoclub.co.uk

Thomas Edison – (February 11, 1847 – October 18, 1931) was an American inventor and businessman. He developed many devices that greatly influenced life around the world, including the phonograph, the motion picture camera and the long-lasting, practical electric light bulb.

Timothy Gallwey – (born 1938 in San Francisco, California) is an author who has written a series of books in which he has set forth a new methodology for coaching and for the development of personal and professional excellence in a variety of fields, that he calls "The inner Game."

Since he began writing in the 1970s his books include: The inner Game of Tennis, The Inner Game of Golf,

The Inner Game of Music, Inner Skiing and The Inner Game of Work.

Anthony "Tony" Peter Buzan – (born 2 June 1942) is an English author and educational consultant.

Buzan popularized the idea of mental literacy and a thinking technique called Mind Mapping earlier used by Leonardo da Vinci and others.

Anthony "Tony" Robbins – (born Anthony J. Mahavoric; February 29, 1960) is an American businessman, author, and philanthropist. He became well known from his infomercials and self-help books: *Unleash the Power Within and Awaken the Giant Within.*

Wayne Dyer – (May 10, 1940 – August 29, 2015) was an internationally renowned author and speaker in the field of self-development. He wrote more than 40 books, 21 of them NYT bestsellers.

His first book, "Your Erroneous Zones" (1976), is one of the best selling books of all time with an estimated 35 million copies sold to date.

GLOSSARY

Aikidoka – student of Aikido

Awase – to blend with or match and Includes both movement and timing

Boken – Japanese wooden sword used for training, usually the size and shape of a katana.

Budo – Budo is a compound of the root bu, meaning war or martial; and do, meaning path or way, often translated as "the way of war", or "martial way", while bujutsu is translated as "science of war" or "martial craft." Budo also gives attention to the mind and how one should develop oneself. Modern budo uses aspects of the lifestyle of the samurai of feudal Japan and translates them to self-development in modern life.

Calibration – to literally measure, used in NLP to describe seeing non-verbal signals in others.

Congruence – is the state achieved by coming together, the state of agreement.

Dojo – is a Japanese term, which literally means "place of the way". Initially, dojos were adjunct to temples. The term can refer to a formal training place for any of the Japanese do arts but typically it is considered the formal gathering place for students of any japanese martial arts style to conduct training, examinations and other related encounters.

Encyclopaedia of Systemic NLP –
http://nlpuniversitypress.com

Foveal Vision – refers to vision in the center of the field of vision, where visual acuity is at its highest.

Hanmi – this is the classic aikido stance that comes from the use of the sword (ken) and spear (jo).

Hara – In the Japanese medical tradition and in Japanese martial arts traditions, the word Hara is used as a technical term for a specific area (physical/anatomical) or energy field (physiological/energetic) of the body, just below the navel.

Iwama – Iwama is located about 100 km northeast of Tokyo and near the city of Mito. Iwama is known for having been the residence of Morihei Ueshiba, the founder of Aikido, from 1942 until his death in 1969 and lends its name to the Aikido of O Sensei and Saito Shihan.

Katana – is a type of Japanese sword and also commonly referred to as a "samurai sword". The katana is characterized by its distinctive appearance: a curved, slender, single edged blade, circular or squared guard, and long grip to accommodate two hands.

Ken – Japanese wooden sword used for training, usually the size and shape of a katana.

Kinaesthetic – refers to the feeling sense and is made up of touch, emotions, movement and balance.

Kokyu – Literally translated as "breath". Probably the equivalent of the Chinese idea of Chi. Difficult to explain but essentially energy that is directed through the body and emanating from the centre. Without Kokyu there is no Aikido. I once asked an Aikido Shihan what he thought the equivalent of Kokyu in life was. He replied it was the utilisation of whatever was around and available to us.

Misogi – is a Japanese mountain ascetic practice of ritual purification. This may be undertaken through exhaustive activities such as extended periods without sleep, breath training, standing under waterfalls, or other methods. Water-misogi may be likened to dousing practices.

Modelling – Behaviour modelling involves observing and mapping the successful processes which underlie an exceptional performance of some type.

NLP – Neuro Linguistic Programming

Polio – Poliomyelitis, often called polio or infantile paralysis, is an acute viral infectious disease spread from person to person. Now mostly eliminated in western cultures.

Rapport – is a term used to describe, in common terms that two or more people feel in sync or on the same wavelength.

Representational Systems – refers to the neurological mechanisms behind the five senses.

Samurai – is the term for the military nobility of pre-industrial Japan.

2nd Position – taking second position involves the ability to step into another person's point of view or perceptual position within a particular situation or interaction and is also known as empathy. It is one of the three perceptual positions utilised in practically every process developed by systemic and NLP new coding and is the essence of emotional intelligence.

Sensei – is a Japanese title used to refer to or address teachers, professors, professionals such as lawyers, doctors, politicians, clergymen, and other figures of authority. The word is also used to show respect to someone who has achieved a certain level of mastery in an art form or some other skill.

Shihan – Senior teacher or Sensei.

Sufism – defined by its adherants as the inner, mystical dimension of Islam. A practitioner of this tradition is generally known as a Sufi.

Takemusu – was the concept developed by O Sensei, Morihei Ueshiba of how the ultimate martial art should be, how his aikido should be, an art, which may harmonise all living beings, and free techniques could be spontaneously executed.

In his later years, O Sensei developed the more spiritual aspects of his art and even adopted the name Takemusu Tsunamori under which he left many paintings and poems.

Tanto – wooden knife

Tori – the person who completes the technique

Uke – the person who is the receiver of the technique

Uptime – a term used to describe a psychological state in which all one's sensory awareness is focussed on the external environment in the here and now.

Yakusa – Japanese mafia also known as Gokudo, are members of traditional organised crime syndicates in Japan.

Yudansha – Anyone holding a black belt (Dan) grade. According to Michael Field Sensei, wearing a black belt and hakama entails certain understanding and responsibility

It is a role based on several different levels; ranging from the physical, to the mental, and also the social, a role that is a conglomeration of skills that have been honed from the first day of training.

Zen – A school of Mahayana Buddihism. The word Zen is from the Japanese pronunciation of the Chinese word Chán which in turn is derived from the Sanskrit word dhyana which can be approximately translated as "meditation" or "meditative state".

APPENDICES

PREDICATES

Visual 'V', see

Angle (perspective), appear, aspect, bright, clarify, clarity, clear, cloud, cognisant, colours, conspicuous, dark, delineate, demonstrate, depict, discern, distinguish, dream, dress up, examine, expose, eye, flash, focus, foresee, glance, glimpse, graphic, hindsight, horizon, idea, illusion, illustrate, image, inspect, look, notice, obscure, observe, obvious, outlook, paint, perception, perspective, picture, pinpoint, preview, reveal, see, scene, scope, screen, scrutinise, short-sighted, show, sight, sketchy, spectacle, survey, vague, view, vision, visualise, watch, witness

Auditory 'A', hear

Accent, alarm, amplify, announce, articulate, ask, boisterous, clear, click, chord, communicate, compose, converse, discuss, dissonant, divulge, earshot, enunciate, gossip, grate, growl, harmonise, hear, hush, inquire, interview, key, listen, loud, mention, muffle, noise, note, oral, proclaim, pronounce, rattle, relate, remark, report, ring, roar, rumour, say, scream, screech, shout, shrill, silence, sing, sound, speak, speechless, squeal, state, static, talk, tell, tone, tune, utter, vocal, voice

Kinaesthetic 'K', feel

Active, affected, angle (fishing), bear, callous, carry, charge, cold, concrete, crash, crawl, emotional, feel, finger, firm, fish for, flow, foundation, gentle, grab, grasp, grip, grope, handle, hanging, hard, hassle, heated, hit, hold, hunch, hustle, impact, impress, irritate, lukewarm, motion, move, muddled, panicky, rub, rush, sensitive, set, settled, shallow, sharpen, shift, shock, smash, soft, softly, solid, sore, sort, stir, stress, strike, stroke, structured, support, tangible, tap, tension, throw, tied, tickle, touch, unbearable, unsettled, warm.

Eye Accessing Cues

As a result of studies, and many hours of observations of people from different cultures and racial backgrounds from all over the world, the following eye movement patterns were identified (Dilts, 1976, 1977; Grinder, DeLozier and Bandler, 1977; Bandler and Grinder, 1979; Dilts, Grinder, Bandler and DeLozier, 1980):

Eyes Up and Left: Non-dominant hemisphere visualization – i.e., remembered imagery (Vr).

Eyes Up and Right: Dominant hemisphere visualization – i.e., constructed imagery and visual fantasy (Vc).

Eyes Lateral Left: Non-dominant hemisphere auditory processing – i.e., remembered sounds, words, and "tape loops" (Ar) and tonal discrimination.

Eyes Lateral Right: Dominant hemisphere auditory processing – i.e., constructed sounds and words (Ac).

Eyes Down and Left: Internal dialogue, or inner self-talk (Ad).

Eyes Down and Right: Feelings, both tactile and visceral (K).

Eyes Straight Ahead but Defocused or Dilated: Quick access of almost any sensory information but usually visual

Eye movements as indicators of specific cognitive processes is one of the most well known, if controversial, discoveries of NLP, and potentially one of the most valuable. According to NLP, automatic, unconscious eye movements, or "eye accessing cues," often accompany particular thought processes, and indicate the access and use of particular representational systems.

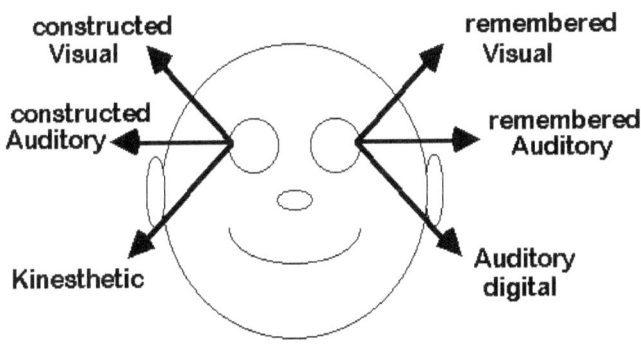

Basic NLP Eye Accessing Cues

A L	**B** R	**C** T	**D** R
E R	**F** R	**G** T	**H** L
I L	**J** T	**K** R	**L** R
M T	**N** R	**O** L	**P** R
Q L	**R** T	**S** T	**T** L
U R	**V** L	**W** L	**X** R

The Alphabet Chart – from page 187

Self Hypnosis

The technique described here is attributed to Elizabeth (Mrs Milton) Erickson. It appears here in the form that it has been used and taught to hundreds of students and clients who have found it both easy to master and highly effective.

Some Basics Premises

This self-hypnosis method is based on the following premises. While there are a number of counter-examples to these notions, they will be of value in understanding and utilizing this process.

An "altered state" of consciousness occurs when you process information outside of your primary representational system.

Hypnosis is a state of concentrated, focused attention.

Going into hypnosis involves turning your attention away from external experience and directing it internally.

You can trust your unconscious mind.

Understanding by the conscious mind is not necessary for change.

Let's consider these ideas one at a time.

Representational Systems and Altered States

We process information (that is, we think) in pictures, sounds and feelings. In Neuro-linguistic Programming, these sensory modalities are referred to as representational systems.

V – The Visual System – The external things we see and the internal images that we create. This includes remembered images *("What does Buckingham Palace look like?")*, constructed images *("What would it look like if it were painted with red and yellow stripes?")*, as well as "live" things we see about us.

A – The Auditory System – The external things we hear, the internal sounds that we create. This includes remembered words or sounds *("Think of the National Anthem")*, imagined words or sounds *("Imagine the National Anthem played on accordions")*, "Self talk", etc. as well as all of the "live" sounds around us.

K – The Kinaesthetic System – The things we feel. These can be actual physical sensations or imagined ones. *Can you imagine being on a beach and feeling sand between you toes?*

Most of us have developed greater proficiency with one or the other of our representational systems though we each use all three of them. Since this is the case, an individual who "thinks" in images wouldn't experience an altered state of consciousness simply by visualizing. However, if that same individual were to experience a preponderance of feelings or sensations, this would be unusual – an alteration of their state of consciousness.

When we talk about altered states, what we're really referring to is processing information in a different manner than usual.

Focused Attention

Stereotypical images of hypnotists holding watches or other fixation devices for clients to stare at are the result of this understanding about hypnosis. If you've ever had the experience of becoming so involved in television or a piece of music or a book, you've experienced this "naturally occurring hypnotic state".

"Going Inside"

The experience of hypnosis is typically an inwardly focused one in which we move away from the environment around us and turn our attention inward.

You can trust your Unconscious Mind

You unconscious mind is "chock full" of resources. In your lifetime of experience, it has learned a great deal and can apply that learning for you in hypnosis. Your conscious mind can only process so much information at one time. Your unconscious mind is not so limited. It can think holographically and is capable of finding better solutions for you than your conscious mind. This process is designed to take full advantage of the power and resourcefulness of your unconscious mind

Understanding by the Conscious Mind is not necessary for Change

In many self-hypnosis procedures, the participants enter a trance and then give themselves suggestions. It seems to me that if my conscious mind knew what to do about the issues that I'm using self-hypnosis for, and then there wouldn't be a need for hypnosis in the first place. In fact, it's often the case that our conscious mind gets in the way. It is the conscious mind that says "I can't..." or "I don't know how to..." or "I'm not smart enough ... ". Some people are surprised to hear this, but consider that if you hear your "self talk" then it isn't unconscious. The process described below is designed to keep the conscious mind occupied so that it won't interfere while your unconscious mind is doing the work.

THE SELF HYPNOSIS TECHNIQUE

Find a Comfortable Position – Get a position that you will be able to maintain easily for the time you are going to be doing this process. It can be sitting or lying down, though sitting is recommended to prevent you from falling asleep. Get yourself centred, just looking in front of you and slightly upwards, breathing slowly and easily. Let yourself relax.

Time – Determine the length of time that you intend to spend and make a statement to yourself about it such as *"I am going into self hypnosis for 20 minutes ..." (or*

however long you want) You will be delighted to discover how well your "internal clock" can keep track of the time for you.

Purpose – Make a second statement to yourself about your purpose in going into self-hypnosis. In this process, we allow the unconscious mind to work on the issue rather than giving suggestions throughout, so our purpose statement should reflect that fact. Here's how I say it:

"... For the purpose of allowing my unconscious mind to make the adjustments that are appropriate to assist me in _____."

Filling in the blank with what you want to achieve such as "developing more confidence in social situations." I know that the text is "wordy" but that's how it came from John Grinder. The actual words aren't nearly as important as the fact your statement acknowledges that you are turning this process over to your unconscious mind.

Exit State – Make a final statement to yourself about the state that you want to be in when you complete the process. Typically in hypnosis, we have heard the idea that you should come back feeling "wide awake, alert and refreshed", but in the real world that may not be what you want. For example, if you are doing your self-hypnosis before bedtime, you may prefer to come out of it "relaxed and ready for sleep". If you're doing it before some project you may want to come out "motivated and full of energy". Simply say to yourself, *"... and when I'm finished, I'm going to feel _____"*.

The Process – Looking in front of you and slightly upwards, notice three things (one at a time) that you see. Go slowly, pausing for a moment on each. It is preferable that they be small things, such as a spot on the wall, a doorknob, the corner of a picture frame, etc. Some people like to name the items as they look at them – "I see the hinge on the door frame". (If you don't know the name for the thing, try "I see that thing over there.").

Now turn your attention to your auditory channel and notice, one by one, three things that you hear. (*You will notice that this allows you to incorporate sounds that occur in the environment rather than being distracted by them.*)

Next, attend to your feeling and notice three things, sensations that you can feel. Again, go slowly from one to the next. It's useful to use sensations that normally are outside of your awareness, such as the weight of your eyeglasses, the feeling of your wristwatch, the texture of your shirt, etc.

Continue the process using two Visual, then two auditory and then two kinaesthetic.

In the same manner, continue (slowly) with one of each.

You have now completed the "external" portion of the process. Now it's time to begin the "internal" part.

Close your eyes.

Bring an image into your mind. Don't work too hard at this. You can construct an image or simply take what comes. It may be a point of light, it may be a beautiful beach, or it could be a pizza. If something comes to you just use it. If nothing comes, feel free to "put something there". Name it as you did above. (I tend to see King Ludwig's castle in Bavaria ... don't ask me why.)

Pause and let a sound come into your awareness or generate one and name it. Although this is technically the internal part, if you should hear a sound outside or in the room with you, it's OK to use that. Remember that the idea is to incorporate things that you experience rather than being distracted by them. Typically, in the absence of environmental sounds, this is where I hear the sound of a Mariachi band. Again, don't ask.

Next, become aware of a feeling and name it. It's preferable to do this internally – use your imagination. (I feel the warmth of the summer sun on my arms) However, as with the auditory, if you actually have a physical sensation that gets your attention, use that. Repeat the process with two images, then two sounds, then two feelings.

Repeat the cycle once again using three images, three sounds, and three feelings.

Completing the Process – It is not unusual to "space out" or to lose consciousness during the process. At first some people think that they've fallen asleep. But generally you will find yourself coming back automatically at the end of the allotted time. This is an indication that you weren't sleeping and that your unconscious mind was doing what you asked of it.

Note: Most people don't get all the way through the process. That's perfectly all right. If you should complete the process before the time has ended, just continue with 4 images, sounds, feelings, then 5 and so on. As for your goals, trust that your unconscious mind is working for you "in the background" while you're doing the process.

Regular Practice Yields Better and Better Results.

WHAT TO DO AND HOW TO DO IT

So what can you do with all of this? How can you use it in "real life", I hear you cry? This is something I am asked by most of the people I train or coach and my response is always to concentrate on one thing at a time, practice and get good at it until it becomes automatic and then choose another thing and practise that until it becomes natural as in the four stages of learning that we talked about earlier.

The initial difficulty with using any of this is that we have automatic responses to situations and those responses are not always the most effective ways to deal with whatever is going on.

For instance when somebody does or says something and we immediately start to defend our selves, loudly and angrily and this will often escalate the situation. We are triggered and driven into action by how we feel, i.e. our emotion that we call anger, frustration or confusion.

Basically we are not in control of our own feelings and our behaviour reflects that. So how can you be prepared enough to automatically respond in a more useful way? Your results originate in your thoughts and what creates your thoughts?

"The answer is you are already programmed to respond in that way. You come into the world as an empty vessel and then get information pumped into you and that's all you know and can act from. We don't know why we make our decisions but it is based on the best we know and crucially the emotion that is evoked and it is sometimes extremely unhelpful in supporting success. Decision is the ultimate power." – Tony Robbins

Next we enter the education system where we are not taught how to shape our beliefs. We are taught to do as we are told, adopt the systems' beliefs and not taught to think entrepreneurially.

By doing these learnt behaviours over and over enough times we can become stuck with limiting beliefs about our selves and what is possible rather than following our heart and dreams. You can, therefore, do the same thing to learn to operate out of a different set of beliefs and install the new behaviours you would prefer to have instead. Stop watching the news and be positive.

A key moment is when you are triggered into the emotional feeling response of anger because once that happens you tend to go down that road. Self-awareness or mindfulness allows you to notice your response and then you can begin to use these "tools" to change your unwanted behaviour.

Better still is to be prepared so that we can automatically respond in the way we want to at that point when we begin to experience the unwanted feeling response. What you want is a way to send the brain down a different pathway so that you can experience the feeling you would prefer to have. This is an example of why being able to manage your state will enable you to perform in an excellent way.

Anchoring – One way to do this is by using the process of Anchoring that we have already discussed, to build positive states, see page 226.

I know trainers, speakers, coaches, managers, parents, and actors and sports people who use anchoring to build positive states that they can use at any time and especially in those situations that previously would have triggered you into an unwanted response.

They build themselves a library of positive states and set up different anchor points like finger and thumb, knuckles or an ear lobe, all of which can be accessed easily and precisely, without being obvious to others and, when pressed will fire different positive states.

Some of the states you can build are:

Relaxation, calmness, happiness, high performance, times of learning or when you performed something well and had a really good feeling afterwards. You can also choose times when you have good energy or humour, whatever floats your boat and helps you get going in a useful way.

If you do some form of exercise, that will cause brain chemical changes that are useful for putting you into a positive state and you can anchor the feelings you get from those changes as well.

The important thing for you to do is be prepared and to know what your outcome is. You are building yourself a toolbox so that, rather than be at the mercy of your own emotions, you can choose how you want to feel by being centered and utilising your anchors. The brain is a muscle and like any other muscle in the body benefits from exercise. You don't need to wait until you have a better job or more money or that special relationship. Why not choose happiness now?

Once your doubts are cleared up you can get to your dream faster than you had thought possible. Anchoring and being centered are excellent ways of managing your feelings and you will find that with regular use your brain will begin to choose those new pathways that you are creating, automatically. That is the nature of how a new habit is built and the ability to be able to do that is the gift of NLP.

Of course you can use anchoring to access a high performance state for such things as presentations, meetings, interviews, sports, negotiations etc. The better state you are in, the better your performance can be. It is the most important thing to do, manage your own state.

Think of all the positive states that would be useful for you in building a high performance state. Access those states one by one, as in the anchoring process, and then stack and fix them by holding your finger and thumb together or holding a knuckle or your ear lobe.

Meditation is another way to manage your state, takes a bit longer obviously and for most people, the main purpose is the reduction of physical and mental stress and to gain a certain degree of peace of mind.

The benefits of meditation and mindfulness practice include an increase in the body's ability to heal, manage depression and anxiety, and move even more towards happiness, relaxation, and emotional balance.

Here's a little piece of mindfulness practice for you:

Chade – Meng Tan says in his book "Search Inside Yourself":

"Focus and follow you're breathing for 10 seconds once every hour. If you forget just start to do it again once you realise you've missed one of those 10 seconds in an hour."

Visualise your own success. Practise the New Behaviour Generator visualisation process every day. It only takes a few minutes.

We are very good at creating pictures in our minds of negative memories or situations as well as running movies of negative scenarios that we think may happen in the future. We then loop this sequence around, maybe adding a bit of negative internal dialogue (self talk). This is a very effective way of building an anxiety state.

Guess what? If you do that on a regular basis it becomes a self-fulfilling prophecy and bad things will happen. Some people call this worrying and stress.

"I am an old man and have known a great many troubles, but most of them never happened." – Mark Twain

Do the New Behaviour Generator and build big, bright, moving and colourful pictures of you succeeding and you will find that you can begin to perform in an excellent way just like the basketball players who visualised themselves scoring with every shot as part of the Chicago research project.

Internal Dialogue. Sometimes our own internal dialogue, i.e. what we are saying to ourselves or voices of others can be very limiting, we sort of beat ourselves up, over and over gradually putting ourselves into negative states. When you notice this and find it difficult to stop that internal dialogue here are some strategies you can use.

Change the qualities of the voice:

- Turn the volume down. If that doesn't work, turn the volume up until it's so loud, becomes unbearable and unrealistic and pops and becomes very humorous

- Change the location of the voice. Have it come from the opposite side, from behind or in front or put it on the end of your big toe

- Change the voice to a cartoon character. Road Runner always works for me. It's difficult to take him seriously

- Play some funny music in the background like circus music or something dramatic like Beethoven's 5th.

Having done all that think about some useful and positive things you can say to yourself and remember tone of voice is important and powerful. Your tone of voice can be pleasant, inviting, motivating and inspiring. Small shifts in tone of voice can be the difference that makes the difference. Actors learn many ways to say the word "yes" so that it can mean yes, maybe or even no.

They can say it so it's a question, a denial, a curse, a blessing etc.

Set yourself goals and well form those goals. Remember the old saying: "Be careful what you ask for because you are likely to get it".

You are giving your brain a target to aim for, a direction to go in and the opportunity to achieve what you want, and that is what your brain does best. Then, always ask yourself for what purpose do you want this? This is the "Why" and as American entrepreneur, author and motivational speaker, Jim Rohn said:

"The bigger the why the easier the how"

Good Luck – and remember what Golfer, Arnold Palmer or was it Gary Player who said:

"The harder I work, the luckier I get"

And I like to think of it as:

"The smarter I work, the luckier I get"

UNIVERSAL PRINCIPLES OF EXCELLENCE

State – accessing high performance states, managing emotions. Thinking creates feelings that determine actions that creates results, so be mindful about what and how you are thinking

Outcome, Awareness, Flexibility – The Success Strategy – for what purpose or why – our values, the hot buttons of motivation

Calibration – awareness of non-verbal signals

Relationship – Rapport, matching and leading, the structure of influence

Perceptual positions – a triple description, different perspectives

Presuppositions – underlying principles

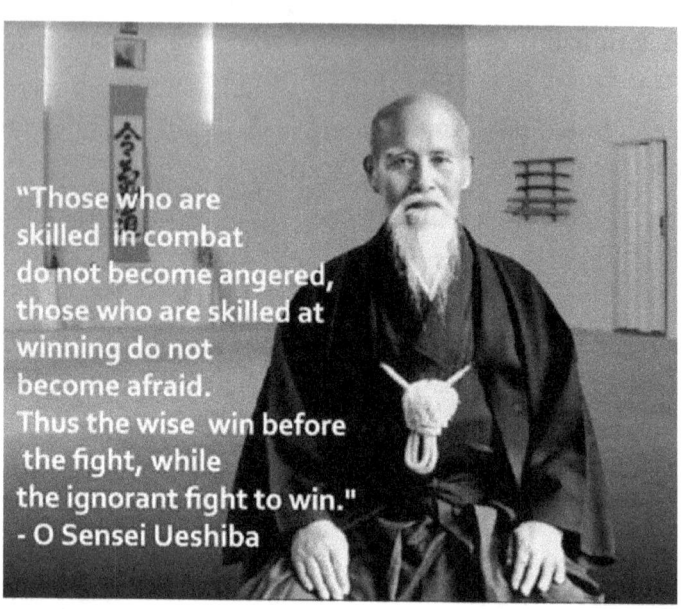

"Those who are skilled in combat do not become angered, those who are skilled at winning do not become afraid. Thus the wise win before the fight, while the ignorant fight to win."
- O Sensei Ueshiba

www.ingramcontent.com/pod-product-compliance
Lightning Source LLC
Chambersburg PA
CBHW052014070526
44584CB00016B/1750